A Writer's Guide to
PERSISTENCE

How to Create a Lasting and Productive Writing Practice

JORDAN ROSENFELD

19 18 17 16   5 4 3 2

Distributed in Canada by Fraser Direct
100 Armstrong Avenue
Georgetown, Ontario, Canada L7G 5S4
Tel: (905) 877-4411

Distributed in the U.K. and Europe by F&W Media International
Brunel House, Newton Abbot, Devon, TQ12 4PU, England
Tel: (+44) 1626-323200, Fax: (+44) 1626-323319
E-mail: postmaster@davidandcharles.co.uk

Distributed in Australia by Capricorn Link
P.O. Box 704, Windsor, NSW 2756 Australia
Tel: (02) 4577-3555

ISBN-13: 978-1-59963-884-3

Edited by *Rachel Randall*
Designed by *Bethany Rainbolt*
Production coordinated by *Debbie Thomas*

Praise for *A Writer's Guide to Persistence*

"In *A Writer's Guide to Persistence* Jordan Rosenfeld offers a gentle, loving nudge not only to novice writers but also to those of us who have been working at writing for most of our lives: You are the only one who can make you stop writing. Be persistent. Remember why you chose writing, and, especially, remember why writing chose you. In short, this book is not only practical, it is also that rare thing that only the best books of craft are, and that is therapeutic. This book will hold a cherished spot in my bookshelves, and whenever I feel the need to be reminded of why I chose this writing life, I will take it down, open it up, and dwell in its loving words. I hope you will do the same."
— Myfanwy Collins, author of *The Book of Laney* and *Echolocation*

"The power of a writer to inspire and connect with other writers is unparalleled. Jordan Rosenfeld's kind but firm voice is the writing teacher we all wish we had and is backed by prodigious talent and output that gives her a seriously earned authority. I was in a slump when I read *A Writer's Guide to Persistence,* and the Work It and Move It sections were just what I needed to persist!" —Maggie May Etheridge, author of *Atmospheric Disturbances*

"At a time when writers feel pushed to build platforms, target markets, and sell huge numbers of books, Jordan Rosenfeld provides a reprieve. *A Writer's Guide to Persistence* offers a safe haven in which to escape from the pressures and concerns of becoming a successful author as well as a chance to recall why we write and why we must, at all costs, continue writing. She helps us remember that if we write for the right reasons, our work will get read. *A Writer's Guide to Persistence* is a must-read for anyone who wants to develop the tenacity to write consistently and successfully." —Nina Amir, best-selling author of *How to Blog a Book* and *The Author Training Manual* (www.ninaamir.com)

ACKNOWLEDGMENTS

While this book is a product of my own persistence, I wouldn't have such inner steel if not for the many mentors I've had along the way: from my first-grade teacher who saw that I was reading above my grade level, to my Opa who gave me the first typewriter I could call my own, to the college professors who told me that I could make it as a writer if I stuck with it, and so many more. I thank my Creative Support Team for cheerleading, hand-holding, doing a crack-job of editing, and talking me down off various ledges, as well as getting me out of my head and into my body—Alegra Clarke, Amy McElroy, Martha Alderson—and the rest of the Scarlet Letter Ladies who pinch-hit as CST members: Becca Lawton, Christina Mercer, Erika Mailman, Julia Park Tracey, Nanea Hoffman, Stephanie Naman, and Tomi Wiley James. And to Cindy Lamothe and Katie Devine, whose conversations about the writing life have helped reinforce the merit of this book.

Also to my circle of dear friends who stick around even after I hermit myself up for months to finish book deadlines: You know who you are.

Deepest gratitude to Phil Sexton for confirming that my ideas were worth pursuing and to Rachel Randall, Editor Extraordinaire, without whom this book would be a whole lot more like a series of journal entries and less a polished book.

And, always, to my husband, Erik, and our son, Ben, who suffer the slings and arrows of living with a writer and still love me.

Table of
CONTENTS

Part Three: **PERSIST**

INTRODUCTION

Some writers persist at the craft of writing—they succeed at publishing, finding an audience, even making a living from their words. But many more do not. Is a penchant for success just something you're born with, like good genes or brown hair? Not at all. Persistence is the key factor, the dividing line, between writers who succeed and writers who merely wish to. It comes not from mental acuity or superstrength but from finding the deep meaning and joy at the root of your writing practice and calling on this joy to get you through the challenges. If you believe in what you're writing, take pleasure in the act of doing so, learn to keep working when it's hard, and put in place a range of strategies to weather the rough patches, you are that much more likely to persist—and thus to succeed.

In my years as a freelance journalist and radio host, during which I interviewed hundreds of writers, I can't tell you how many times I heard the phrase, "I am not as successful as I would like to be." This came from not only emerging writers but from *New York Times* bestselling authors as well. How can this be? The fear of not being "successful enough" is conjured from the ego's dauntless quest for more, for better, for whatever is "over there." To the ego, happiness exists outside of the self, and therefore, so does success. I'm here to reassure you that you can be happy with your writing practice right now, in this moment, if you choose to be. Moreover, taking this attitude and the practices recommended in this book will prepare the ground for your writing success. Thus when you do snag that publishing deal or grow your audience into a vibrant community of eager readers, you won't find yourself empty, discouraged, or wishing for a different kind of success.

A Writer's Guide to Persistence is a tool kit to support you through the unique challenges of the literary art so that you can create a sustainable, long-term writing practice without being swayed by the constant changes, negative criticism, and doubts that come with the territory.

This books aims to help you feel comforted, supported, and less alone, and also offers practical tricks to free you from detrimental habits. It aims to get you back on your feet after a variety of crises and common writer calamities so that you can do the important writing you are meant to do and nourish your writer's spirit. If you are called to write, you must take it seriously, and this book can help you do just that.

This book was inspired by the many, many talented writers I know, published in myriad ways: by their own hands, through a small press, or with a big publisher. They are all human, full of fears and doubts just like the rest of us, but also motivated, persistent, and hardworking—qualities that count toward cultivating success.

The concept of success has been co-opted by the flash-bang spirit of that tiny percent of writers who achieve rock star, billionaire status. It's been twisted to be synonymous with *fame, fortune,* and *world renown.* While I can't argue that those conditions do add up to success, there are many, many other factors that don't have anything to do with the approval of another person (or publication) but that lead to fulfillment as a writer. As long as you focus on an outcome you have no control over, you will come to your writing with conflicted feelings that range from frustration to despair. And focusing on what you can't control will hamper your ability not only to reach for those larger goals of success but also to do the very thing you came here to do: sit down and write.

There is a fine line between the creation of art for its own sake and sharing that art with an audience. We live in a culture that says fame and fortune await anyone willing to work hard enough. But not everyone will be J.K. Rowling or Stephen King. Once you surrender to this truth, you can see what is on the other side of fame and fortune; i.e., all the worthy reasons you started writing in the first place, including joy, purpose, expression, connection, discovery, journeying, catharsis, and having a deep, rich, and meaningful writing practice.

If this book can do anything for you, it can remind you that no situation is bad enough that it deserves to steal your joy or right to write. This book is a refuge for dealing with the challenges and woes that all writers face. It helps you focus instead on making your art—on *writing*—which then gives you something important to share with an audience. By coming from a joyful place of authenticity and doing consistent work, your writing will stand a chance of rising above to reach many others. Read the chapters in order, or choose those chapters that speak to your particular challenges.

Above all, be persistent.

JORDAN E. ROSENFELD

Part One
PRACTICE

chapter 1
LOVE THE JOURNEY

"*Making the work you want to make means finding nourishment within the work itself.*"
—DAVID BAYLES AND TED ORLAND, FROM *ART & FEAR: OBSERVATIONS ON THE PERILS (AND REWARDS) OF ARTMAKING*

Do you remember a time when you felt like words ran in your veins instead of blood; when ideas that were knocking around in your head crystallized on a crisp, white journal page; when you couldn't wait for a few minutes alone to jot down a molten thought you'd held onto all day at work? At some point in your journey as a writer, you have likely experienced the exhilaration, satisfaction, relief, release, and joy of being a wordsmith and have hungered for more.

While each of us writes for different reasons, most of the writers I've known share one thing in common: Writing is an integral part of their lives. For some, it's even their life's purpose. For others, it's an important or necessary part of expressing themselves, connecting with others, and making meaning. Writing is an art, but I like to refer to it as a "craft"—which holds the possibility for improvement and change. Writing allows you to delve deep into yourself and to connect with your fellow humans in a very powerful way, which often leads to new corridors of knowledge and understanding.

But life is not a straight line. Things get in the way of the joy and flow: responsibilities, family obligations, stress, hurtful words, competition, overwhelm, internal critics, and more. So while the aphorism "love the journey, not the destination" is so familiar it's become cliché, I'm saying it here because it is crucial to your success. At the end of your life, I can't imagine that you will regret taking more time to write and to practice the art you love. The act of writing is a meaningful one. Writers are prone to forgetting the other benefits of the art, because the lure of reward, praise, and outside approval always beckons and sometimes pulls us off our path. We get caught up in the minutiae, urged on by internal demons that suggest we need to achieve more, faster, and with wilder success.

FAVOR PROCESS OVER PRODUCT

When I was twenty-six I took a great leap into the unknown and attended a low-residency masters degree program in creative writing at Bennington College, Vermont. As an only child with parents who worked full-time, I'd felt lonely if I wasn't carrying a notebook or letter-writing paper with me at all times. Thus, as an adult, it made sense to pursue a full-immersion experience that might also get me a decent job in a field I loved. I borrowed tens of thousands of dollars in student loans, plus the cost of books and airfare, and flew away from my husband twice a year, from California to Vermont, to attend two-week sessions. Each day of these sessions was packed with lectures, critique workshops, and fervent discussions about writing and literature. I came home positively burning with creativity and literary philosophies, and driven to aspire to the words of our program director, who quoted Alec Baldwin's memorable words in *Glengarry Glen Ross*—"Always be closing"—and urged us to put our best effort into all our work. My brain was so full that I could do nothing but unspool it onto the page in the months between the session I had just attended and the next one.

When people asked me what I hoped to do with my MFA, I began to realize that the answer was quite different from the reason I'd begun pursuing it: "To write more," I'd say.

"But don't you want to teach or write text books or something?"

I *thought* I wanted to do those things, but quickly it became clear that writing *to create* was the pulse that beat loudest inside me. In going through the program, I realized that there was profound meaning in apprenticing myself to an art that was already my great love. What I took away from that program, more than anything else, was that writing is not just a means to an end but a way of life, of processing information and experience, and of expressing oneself on a regular basis. Where would we be without the powerful work of writers like Plato, Shakespeare, Maya Angelou, or Ann Patchett? The single consistent "magic ingredient" I took away from all the writers who taught or lectured to us—including such noted and award-winning writers as Sven Birkerts, Amy Bloom, Joyce Maynard, Rick Moody, and many more—was that hard work coupled with a deep passion for the art (versus laboring toward an end product) led to more success than any other formula. I graduated with certainty that it is meaningful to write for reasons other than financial gain and publication.

The outcomes, or products, of your work—completed writing, publication, acclaim, or awards—are merely proof of the different stages you've reached in this wonderful calling.

Alongside being a writer, I've now been teaching writing in one form or another for over a decade, and time and again I see writers struggle with a variety of harsh voices, challenges, and demons. The difference between the happy-but-struggling writer and the writer who gives up or falls into despair is that the happy one finds ways to love the journey and knows that a writing practice is worthy because the act of putting words on the page is a transformative, profound, important, meditative, and sometimes bold process.

If you hope to keep writing your entire life, you *must* love it. If your love for the act of writing has wilted like a bloom in the light of practical reality—if exterior or interior critical voices or the obligations of your daily life are keeping you from enjoying it—it's time to reassess and remember why you started this enterprise in the first place. You owe it to yourself.

I'll bet that if you're reading this book, writing has been many things for you: a haven, a place to speak freely, a safe space, a corridor of discovery, a way to challenge yourself, a journey into deeper parts of yourself and subjects that matter to you, and maybe even just something that you've always been good at, that you can or would like to make a living at. If you're reading this book, you're well on your way to claiming, or reclaiming, those things.

MAKE NO EXCUSES

This book will be gentle and kind and compassionate. It will give you tips for coping, strategies to stretch yourself, and reminders of your worth and value. But it will not coddle you. It will not support your excuses or reasons not to write. It will not treat you as a victim of circumstances.

There is really only one true aphorism in writing: Writers must write. How you do it, where, when, and why are all up to you. But if you say you want to be a writer, and especially if your aim is to publish, you won't get there by talking or dreaming alone.

Every writer has had the same or similar demands on his time as you do. I once interviewed author Ingrid Hill, a published mother of twelve children—that's right, *twelve*—who not only wrote and published but had just won a grant from the National Endowment for the Arts. Everyone has some variation of demands stemming from work, spouses, family members, children, carpool schedules, health challenges, needy pets, ailing relatives, challenging friends, mortgages and assorted bills to pay, and so on. Excuses are a way of keeping yourself "safe" from the demands of a writing practice. Writing isn't just time-consuming; it can make you feel vulnerable and raw, and can bring on intense emotions. Suddenly, you're exposing yourself. People are seeing and hearing you as you really are. No doubt you feel a certain responsibility for sending your words into the world and even sometimes for just committing certain intense thoughts to paper.

And yet: Writers must write.

Writers are the people who find a way, no matter what, to keep writing, polishing, and persisting. You are no different than all the other writers in the world.

No excuses. No one will do it for you. Your writing practice is in your hands.

WORK IT

1. Why do you write? Have you ever sat down and asked yourself this question?

Take out a notebook or open a new document on your computer or tablet. Make a free-form list—that is, don't stop and think too much about what you're writing—and write from the gut. No reason is better than another. Write as many reasons as you can until you feel done.

Now ask yourself: What are the top five reasons?

2. Compose a second "negative" list. What stands in the way of your writing? What fears, habits, beliefs, or critical voices are trying to drown your desire to write?

For each item on the "negative" list, use your top five reasons for writing to "cancel out" the negative. In other words, use your reasons to trump your fears. Here's an example.

> NEGATIVE: I'm afraid of being criticized or rejected.
> A TOP FIVE REASON I WRITE: I want to make a difference to others through my words.

You may find that your fears and doubts are simply the mirrored reflection of your desires and that the cost of not pursuing your writing dreams will be far worse than any fear you might hold. When you reframe a negative in a positive light, it's much harder to hold onto it.

3. If you don't feel like writing at this moment, meditate. Sit quietly with your eyes closed, focus on your breathing, and let the words in this chapter enter you. The goal of this meditation is to make you feel centered, inspired, and ready to write.

MOVE IT

Part of sustaining a healthy writing practice is taking good care of the vehicle you're in—your body. The job you are tasked with can be treacherous for your body, and it's often difficult to stay limber when you're anchored to a desk, so it's crucial that you get up and move not only after a long time spent sitting but at regular intervals during the writing process. Any time you've been sitting for an hour or more, your body makes preparations to go into "shutdown" mode—essentially, it's preparing for death. Yikes!

Pause to take a quick walk in a beautiful, calm, and quiet place near your home or office, whether that's on your lunch break or after several hours spent writing. As you walk, focus on feeling your feet on the earth. Improve your posture by lifting your chest and chin. Tell yourself you're on a journey, you're walking a path, and you are right where you need to be. Allow this chapter's message to sink into you and change your writing, your self.

When you return, do one thing for your writing self that fills you with happiness, whether it is writing related (cracking open a fresh Moleskine notebook) or just pleasurable (breaking off a chunk of chocolate to enjoy as a snack).

PERSISTENCE IS PERSONAL:
Your Writing Reflects Your Self
by Martha Alderson, author of The Plot Whisperer books

The relationship you have with your writing directly reflects the relationship you have with yourself.

Love your writing. Love yourself.

Hate yourself. Hate your writing.

When you write fiction or memoir, your journey as a writer often mirrors your character's development. In the case of a memoir, it does so literally, as you are your book's narrator. As your character is stripped of everything or sheds an old personality or belief system, you also suffer anguish and doubt. I've consulted with writers who experienced major health complications in the middle of writing a particularly personal story and struggled to get well. I've experienced my own dark times, which always reflect how I'm feeling about the journey of writing: It always translates to the journey of life and the

Universal Story. As I say in my book *The Plot Whisperer*, "All of us face antagonists and hurdles, hopes and joys, and by meeting these challenges we can transform our lives. I have come to believe that every scene in every book is part of a Universal Story that flows throughout our lives, both in our imaginations and in the reality that surrounds us."

When I discovered how the Universal Story works, I came to understand that I'm not a victim and that the events that happen to me as a writer aren't out to hurt me. In fact, it's quite the opposite: Writing invites self-exploration and evolution. As I dig for meaning in my words and stories, and find what's true for my characters, somehow I always manage to dredge up wounds from the past and unearth parts of myself I never expected to dredge up. In striving to understand my character's inner motivations, I discover many of my own. As I experiment with my character's fluctuating emotions, I challenge myself to act differently.

The deeper into a story I write, the more perilous the journey always becomes. After years of starting and stopping and starting again, I finally learned how to bypass the drama, the struggle, the angst—and that's through surrender. Today, with each writing challenge I face, I find out more about who I am, and through my writing, I heal myself.

To love the journey, I must separate from my ego, expectations, dreams, and desires and detach from the outcome. To feel truly alive, action is required of me at this moment. Not someday in the future—*right now*. I need to write strong. To write with clarity. To take responsibility for my writing. To show up, face my fear, and continue writing in spite of it. Facing oneself is never easy. Loving oneself can be even harder. When we do, the emptiness inside us fills.

Live on the edge. You won't fail. The Universal Story always delivers exactly what you need so that you can become who you intended to be on your way to liberation.

When I let myself be who I am and love who I am, I delight in the transformation in and around me. I love the words I write right now. There is never an end, simply a new beginning. I write without judgment and in ways that bring me pleasure.

We all long to be heard. I've learned that longing for a future with a prize-winning, best-selling story leads to heartache. Give up the illusion that you have any control over the future. Rather than longing to be heard, long to hear. Listen for words whispered from the other side of the veil. Feel an easy joy about your writing. Separate your worries about what comes after for when you've finished the book, and simply listen to your heart, in this moment, right now.

chapter 2

CREATE A PRACTICE

"*We are made to persist. That's how we find out who we are.*"

—TOBIAS WOLFF, FROM *IN PHARAOH'S ARMY: MEMORIES OF THE LOST WAR*

I love the word *practice* for its versatility. As a verb, it exhorts you to perform an exercise or skill regularly "in order to improve or maintain one's proficiency," according to *Merriam-Webster*. As a noun, it is "the application or use of an idea or method." To become the writer you hope to be, you must both *engage in* and *sustain* a practice. The great artists of the past apprenticed themselves to a master and practiced their art with the main goal of honing their craft. In today's world, you will benefit from engaging in a similar relationship to your writing. The moment you see it as a "practice" that derives from an authentic place inside you, you step outside the bounds of success and failure and enter a wholly new, deeper territory in which everything you do for and with your writing is part of a greater sum. No words or work are ever wasted. No failure is ultimate; instead everything is another step further on the path of your writing *practice*.

Nearly a decade ago, in my freelance journalism career, I worked on a story for the *Petaluma Magazine* interviewing dozens of local visual artists. One woman's comments have stuck with me across the years:

When asked what it took to produce a final painting that satisfied her, her answer was "Miles of canvas." I could envision those miles, logged at all hours of the day and night; I could picture her body as the engine for her vision, paint splattered across her studio and brow. Often countless "draft" paintings went into the one she finally called complete. It's much the same for a writer producing drafts of a book or story. Her words encouraged me deeply; they helped me see that everything counts as long as you choose to see it in that light. The value of your writing practice is ultimately up to you. And once you know what that value is, no one can take it from you through rejection, criticism, or competition.

Chapter one encouraged you to love the journey on the way to your destination. Here I'll teach you the four key steps to building what I call a "Writer's Code," which serves as the foundation of your writing practice.

BUILD A WRITER'S CODE

1. What is the value of your writing?

Your writing means a lot to you because of what you bring to it—passion, clarity, joy—and because it will elicit these and other feelings in your audience. Determining the value of your writing *to you*—why you do it—is the first step in building an unshakable Writer's Code that you can return to when the doubts come to harangue and hassle you. This is the most personal step of all. Some people in your life may wish that you made a bigger income from your writing (or *any* income at all), or that you would "make something" of yourself after pursuing a degree, or that your writing gave *them* something to be proud of. It's easy to get caught up in thinking about what others want or expect from your writing practice. If your burning reason to write is because it makes you happy or releases the wild voices from your head or helps you analyze the world around you, *you are exactly where you are supposed to be.* You must learn to please yourself in the process of your practice or you will become vulnerable to discouragement, despair, and giving up. At the end of the day, "writing must be its own reward," as Anne Lamott famously said.

You may also desire to have an audience, wild success, and fame. As I said earlier, these shouldn't be the only reasons you write, but they are valuable desires as long as they are rooted to a powerful, authentic place inside you. Desiring fame and fortune for the sake of it often leads to disappointment. But there's absolutely nothing wrong with wanting your work to be read by a large, accepting public and to entertain, educate, or connect. The more you love the actual work of writing and write what you really love to write, the more likely you are to achieve your writing dreams.

So it's time to work. Take out your notebook or tablet and get ready to answer a question in each of the following steps, starting with the one below.

WRITE NOW: *What is the value of your writing? Refer back to chapter one and your top five reasons to write. For each item on your list, spend a minimum of five minutes journaling, going into greater detail about that reason. Seeing the reasons behind your work can go a long way toward empowering you as a writer.*

2. What is your writing rhythm?

Once you're clear on what your writing means to you and why it matters, you will benefit from taking a look at your writing rhythm. I've come to believe that every writer has an inner "momentum"—when your creative energy is at its peak—that is most effectively translated at a particular time of day or night, or under certain conditions. Some writers are morning people; others call the midnight hours their most creative time. Some writers need to be in nature, or away from people, or in the center of a bustling environment they can happily tune out, such as a café.

If you have a family, you are often forced to work around spouses and children, and you might also have a full- or part-time job to juggle. You need to know when your creative mind has the most energy—you'll take this information into account in later chapters as you learn how to manage time and determine when you get the most out of your writing. You will learn to avoid working against yourself or forcing creative time out of yourself when you're least likely to have the energy.

And even though you won't always be free to write at your magic hour, knowing when that hour occurs is an important part of your practice. Down the road you'll learn how to either carve out the time to write when you're at your best or to build your writing muscles to write whenever you have free time.

WRITE NOW: *When are you at your most vigorous and ready to write? What time of day is that? How long do you generally need? When are you at your most spent and tired? What environments best facilitate your creativity? Do you need chaos or isolation? Music or silence? Long stretches of time or quick bursts?*

3. What are you willing to risk?

As a writer you may continue on a comfortable and familiar path, taking measured steps toward your goals. It's perfectly valid and even wise to do so. And yet, as in all things, sometimes risk is required of you in order to grow further or reach a new level of accomplishment or understanding of the craft. But only *you* know what an acceptable level of risk is *for you*.

Another way to define risk is as a "next step" in your journey. If your end goal is to be published but you've never shown your work to another soul, then a logical next step is to seek out and receive critiques. (There are some wonderful sites for finding critique partners—more on that in chapter sixteen—but if you already have a set of trusted readers in your life, use them.) In your pursuit of feedback, it's wise to seek it in a way that is likely to be helpful rather than harmful. You might take a course or turn to a trusted colleague whom you know can deliver critique in an honest but supportive way (as opposed to the more "blunt truth" school of feedback, which isn't for everyone).

If you wish to teach writing or write more academic works, your logical next step might be to pursue a higher degree of education; this step might scare you, but furthering your education is always worth pursuing. Or if you wish to hone your craft, your next step might be to go to a conference, mingle with fellow writers, attend sessions and classes, and sit down in front of agents and editors. It's important to know where your line is and to not cross your risk threshold if you aren't ready. A positive risk leads to growth and new opportunities, and should bring a thrill of possibility. When you take a risk you aren't ready for, you will feel anxious and overwhelmed, and you will set yourself up for discouragement. Sometimes the gleaming promise of reward outshines the cost of the risk, and when that reward doesn't pay out it can be especially disappointing. If this happens, then the risk probably pushed you past your threshold; it's a sign that the risk was too far too soon, and that you should turn back, regroup, and attempt a healthier risk—a logical next step that has the ability to stretch you in the right ways.

WRITE NOW: *What risks can you take that will allow you to stretch and grow? What is a logical next step for you to take in your writing practice or career? What risks are likely to discourage you and lead to despair? Are any of your "next steps" too ambitious? (Revisit and evaluate your answers once a year. As you continue to take small risks, you'll find that your answers have changed since the last time you viewed them, and that will give you the confidence to make creative leaps.)*

4. Who is your creative support team?

All writers go through difficult times. Painful growth is a real and necessary part of your maturation as a writer, but these challenges are not comfortable and can be downright agonizing. I (and every writer I've ever talked with) have experienced deep rejections and setbacks, times when I thought I might never write again, and times when I could only hear "the negative" and not a single compliment. Your goal is to learn to rely on your foundation and to use the tips and strategies outlined in this book to help you through the rough patches on your own if need be. But ultimately even the sturdiest writer needs emotional support and camaraderie. It's a lonely art, one that most writers do in solitude, with few eyes looking in to see how it's going. When people do ask about your work, it's often with well-meaning but unhelpful questions that can cause you to feel like a failure: "What have you published?" or "How many books have you sold?"

What you need is what I call a "Creative Support Team."

Believe it or not, you may already have a Creative Support Team without realizing it. First, look to your family and friends, the nonwriters in your life. Do you know which ones will cheerlead and champion you when you come to them discouraged? Even the most sympathetic friend, spouse, or parent might unintentionally say an unhelpful thing like "Time will heal all wounds" or "You'll get over it." Or worse, "Maybe it just wasn't meant to be." No matter how much you love these people, they are not the ones you need to turn to when the hard times strike. You need people who will, as I have come to refer to it, "talk you off the ledge."

My personal ledge is the place where a harsh criticism or a poorly timed rejection can temporarily convince me that I shouldn't bother pursuing that avenue of publication despite the fact that I have come so close or that I have received as much praise as rejection. There are a handful of trusted comrades I turn to when I reach this place, and no one else. I don't call my parents. I don't even call some of my closest friends. I call on the members of my Creative Support Team. For the record, these people don't know they are a team—many of them don't even know each other. But they do know me—my writing rhythms and insecurities and tantrums—and they know which words will soothe and bolster me.

I recommend having one nonwriter as part of your Creative Support Team, for those days when you just want someone who loves you to throw her literal or figurative arms around you and rally you toward a better mood. Then, of course, you want at least one writer on your team who knows what it's like to be in the trenches, an equal who's trudging the same path you are traveling down in one way or another. And, if possible, it's nice to have a mentor—someone further down the path than you are or someone who has achieved a writing goal you are interested in achieving, who can remind you that your persistence will pay off.

One of my dear friends, Erika Mailman, author of the novels *The Witch's Trinity* and *Woman of Ill Fame*, has been a constant beacon of support and persistence in my life. Six months after my son was born, when I felt I'd lost my muscle for writing, Erika was the one to tell me that the meager pages I was producing at the time were worth pursuing. She cheered me on and gave me feedback and confidence that I could be both mother and writer, and those rough pages eventually went on to be my first published novel, *Forged in Grace*. Similarly I try to show the same kind of support to my critique partner, Amy, also one of my closest friends, when discouragement or doubt gets her down. We often share woes over the spin bike at the gym and text each other daily encouragement.

WRITE NOW: *Who are the members of your Creative Support Team? Who is your biggest nonwriting champion (or champions)? Who among your writing comrades do you feel safest with? Who are your trusted mentors?*

If you don't currently have a champion, imagine what your "ideal" champion would be like.

> 1. *Make a list of the qualities you feel you need in a writing champion. Go on for as long as you want; after all, you're inventing this perfect person.*
> 2. *When you're feeling stuck or discouraged, use your skill as a writer to give yourself a pep talk from the point of view of this imaginary champion. You may be surprised to find that even a "fictional" pep talk from a made-up person has the power to move you out of a negative place and back to writing freely.*

WORK IT

After you've completed each of the exercises in this chapter, you'll have a rough draft of your Writer's Code. Now you can create a visual sheet of your Code that you'll put somewhere handy (perhaps inside a notebook, over your desk, or in a closet you open daily) so you can return to it again and again. Think of it as a contract with yourself that you will renew every six months. As you commit or recommit to your writing journey, any of these details may change.

[NAME]'S WRITER'S CODE

On this day, [date], I state to myself that I write because [list values—as many as you like].

My best writing rhythms are [at your appointed times of day/night and in your optimal conditions].

I will take the following risks [your goals/risks here], but will never extend beyond my comfort zone.

When I struggle, I will turn to my Creative Support Team: [names].

When you're done, print it out, put it up where you can see it, and take it seriously.

MOVE IT

Almost every chapter in this book has a suggestion for moving your body and keeping yourself healthy and your "vehicle" in excellent shape. My friend Amy, who is both a writer and a yoga instructor, taught me to use "stretch breaks."

Breaks aren't just a good idea, they really make a difference; a 2012 Towers Watson global workforce study revealed that people who take breaks from work every ninety minutes were 30 percent more focused. And those who worked beyond forty hours per week and at a more continuous pace felt worse about their jobs, their productivity, and their bodies.

That's why, when Amy and I are both working, we'll text each other, "Stretch break!" (We try to arrange these breaks in advance specifically to enlist each other's support.) When you can, enlist a Creative Support Team member to help remind you.

So here's a golden rule: Every twenty to ninety minutes during extended periods of sitting, give yourself a stretch break.

Remember that stretches need not be deep. Don't go past your comfort zone or go too long; as little as ten seconds is enough to be effective.

One of my favorite stretches for writers is to interlace your fingers, then face your palms out and push your arms out as straight as they will go without pain. Try to soften your shoulder blades down and back toward your tailbone and gently pull in your belly toward your spine so you get a nice stretch.

chapter 3

AWAKEN YOUR AUTHENTICITY

"A man sees in the world what he carries in his heart."
—JOHANN WOLFGANG VON GOETHE, FROM *FAUST*

To begin this chapter I draw upon the whimsical wisdom of Dr. Seuss, who wrote in his authentic, unparalleled, memorable voice, "Today you are You, that is truer than true. There is no one alive who is Youer than You."

Authenticity is a key part of your writing voice and your impact on readers. The irony about authenticity is that often you are the last person to figure out what is authentic about yourself. Similarly you may not yet know what your voice is—part of the journey is learning to determine that—but I guarantee that others could identify the "you-ness" of you if asked. I always take it as a compliment when someone hears a song or reads a quote or a book and says, "This made me think of you," or buys me a gift that is so magnificently perfect for me. This tells me that I possess unique qualities that others can identify.

As a writer, you will (and must) learn to distinguish an authentic voice. Or you may already be aware of your sensibility and wish to whittle it into new shapes. In this chapter, I want you to think about what that voice is or might be. I guarantee there is a you-ness to your writing. Defining elements distinguish your writing from that of your best friend (or arch enemy), your teachers, best-selling authors you admire, or even me. And beneath that, there are elements that are remarkably, indelibly, magnificently you, which no other writer on the planet possesses, because these elements only came into being with the rise of your mind. It's easy to believe that someone else has a more interesting voice, a better way of telling a story, a more compelling handle on language, or even just better material to work with, but the fact is, how and what other people write has very little bearing on your writing. What's your voice? What are your themes? How do sentences sing to you? What kinds of characters do you carve out of the ether of creativity and shape on the page?

If you have any doubt, let me remind you:

Your voice is worthy of being read
- even if you struggle to find it.
- even when it's so soft you aren't sure you can hear it.
- even when it seems to shift and change before your eyes.
- even if you think nobody is listening.

FIND YOUR VOICE

If, however, you still aren't sure of the composition of your voice, the following are some tips for finding it.

In seeking your voice, look to your obsessions and desires: that which haunts you and keeps you up at night. Think of the books you like, the shows you watch, the music that evokes deep emotion within you. The way words stick in your inner ear and the rhythms of your prose combine and manifest in your voice. As do the dialects you're familiar with and the kinds of conversations you are drawn to eavesdrop upon. Voice is an amalgam of your tastes, your interests, your terrors, and your deepest desires.

You may have also heard voice described as "style." Just as you have a style in the way you clothe yourself and arrange your home, you style your words, and, more important, your thoughts, in very specific ways. But the deepest contribution to your voice is your personal themes.

Mine Your Personal Themes

Writers are incredibly impressionable creatures. That is, we take in, hold, absorb, and then mutate the experiences that happen to and around us—and then put them on the page. By pulling from the roots of your formative years as well as from the events of last week, you can find recurring characters, settings, tones, and moods if you learn to see them. You already hold inside you all the words, characters, and settings you need to write thousands of pages.

But don't take my word for it; consider this quote from Albert Camus, from the introduction to his *Lyrical and Critical Essays*: "Every artist is undoubtedly pursuing his truth. If he is a great artist, each work brings him nearer to it, or at least, swings still closer toward this center, this buried sun where everything must one day burn."

Camus was a man of metaphor, of course, but what he means is that you already have a "buried sun"—a treasure chest, really—of language, love, life experience, themes, and more either waiting to be excavated and revealed or molded into shape. It doesn't mean everything you write must be about you or that you must follow to the letter the famous writer's axiom "Write what you know." To write what you know means to write what compels and fascinates you. For example, when I attended my masters in writing program at Bennington College, my professors—all of them published authors—helped me see that I continually repeated certain themes in my work. In fact, Alice Mattison suggested that I could call my collection of stories *Bad Mothers and Absent Fathers*.

To this day, though I write about all kinds of subjects that compel me (everything from healing to dark family secrets), at the root of all my fiction are themes of dysfunctional parenting and parenthood. This is not to say that I actually had a bad mother and an absent father—I could have gleaned these themes just as easily from the copious after-school specials I watched, which usually featured children from broken homes, and the novels about orphans that I loved reading. People who claim to be able to heal and people who have had psychic experiences (neither of which have happened to me) also fascinate me, and those themes make their way into my work often. What my mentors helped me see was that by understanding my themes, I could learn to write about them differently, in new ways, with new eyes and better results, and thus consciously mold my voice. (See more in the "Work It" section of this chapter.)

Use Your Experience

Finding your voice also means writing about the areas of your expertise: your job, your hobbies, the topics you have a vested interest in. Some of the best novels have derived from work authors do in their daily lives. Rene Denfeld, who works as a criminal investigator with death row inmates, wrote a powerful novel, *The Enchanted*, that is set in a prison and features characters drawn from the real work she does. Rebecca Lawton's novel *Junction, Utah* draws largely from her work as one of the first female river guides in the Grand Canyon back in the seventies. In your own work, you can draw on your experience as a teacher, a plumber, or a therapist—or whatever occupation you have. Your life informs your work, fleshes it out, gives it taste, color, and full-bodied emotion. If you sit in a room all day, every day, and try to generate material, you may find yourself running a bit dry. Sure, your imagination can come into play, but I believe there is no better material for your writing than what you experience. Therefore, to write what you know also means to "write what you have experience with." And, yes, you can go out and *obtain* experience in order to write about it. The novelist Jean Hegland once told us in a writing workshop I took that she was training to become certified as a midwife in order to write about it accurately. I know writers who have learned how to ride a unicycle, lived on the streets, learned how to bake, and more just to bring authenticity to their work.

Is there some activity you've always wanted to try, some skill or profession you've always wanted to learn? Do it in service of your writing, and you'll have the best excuse ever: "I'm doing this for my art."

Explore Your Vulnerability

Real, memorable, authentic writing may look different for each person, but it can only exist in the presence of vulnerability. To show your real self and access your true voice, you have to pull down the veil of illusion and write in a way that lays bare your mind, your heart, your secrets, and your longings. This is an act of claiming yourself and saying: *This is me, and I won't pretend to be anyone else.* Most people I know, myself included, read to find connection, validation, and understanding in the words of others. Donna Tartt says novels are written "by the alone for the alone." Ultimately the best way to reach anyone is to be vulnerable.

But vulnerability comes with anxiety for many. (See later chapters on how to handle criticism, rejection, taboo, and sabotage.) The key is to remember that your vulnerability touches others' vulnerable places and illuminates them. It bears witness for those who can't do so on their own behalf. Think of the times you've read a line, a quote, a whole book even, when you felt seen, heard, and validated by an author you've never met. Thanks to the vulnerability of others, you may find permission inside yourself to be real and open, too.

This past year I've been reading a lot of personal essays published in such journals as *The Rumpus*, *The Manifest-Station*, and *Full Grown People*. The bravery and beauty of people sharing their stories has given me permission to do the same, to write about difficult subjects in a way that I have found healing as well as inspiring. This new permission to be vulnerable is now infusing itself into all aspects of my writing—I'm weaving more personal emotion into my fiction and telling the truth more plainly.

I like to remember what social scientist and author Brenè Brown says: "Vulnerability is the birthplace of innovation, creativity, and change."

Write Like Yourself (and Avoid Comparison)

If you're like most writers I know, you've probably experienced a feeling similar to this: *After reading X Author's work, I never want to write again!*

At one point or another, most of us suffer from envy, desiring to write like other talented writers. And it's understandable—the literary landscape is rich with a symphony of voices and resonant with talent.

One of my best friends, Amy, wrote poetry in college about one of her favorite topics: the natural world. She told a teacher: "I want to write a poem about leaves, but that's been done so many times."

The teacher wisely said, "But every poem about leaves is different. Write *your* poem about leaves."

Another friend of mine, Nanea, who writes powerful essays, confessed, "I always feel my life is so vanilla that I don't have anything interesting to say." And then she proceeded to send me an essay about the absurdity of death and the resilience of the human spirit in which "vanilla" never even made an appearance.

This is all to say that you are not always the best person to judge your uniqueness (especially if you're feeling low or insecure). But you are the only one who can make a difference in the quality of your writing. Only you can seek and capture and hone that which makes your writing special.

When you doubt your voice, speak to yourself the way you would a best friend struggling to value herself. Says Anne Lamott, "I doubt that you would read a close friend's early efforts and, in his or her presence, roll your eyes and snicker. I doubt that you would pantomime sticking your finger down your throat. I think you might say something along the lines of, 'Good for you. We can work out some of the problems later, but for now, full steam ahead!'" You wouldn't be mean to your friend if she asked you to assess her work, and you also wouldn't encourage her to stop or abandon meaningful pursuits. When you hear the voices saying you aren't good enough and you don't have anything to say, talk them down. Remind them that you are the only one who can write the way you do. Your voice is worthy. Your voice is unique.

Discover Your Personal Lexicon

Recently I was surprised to discover, from responses to a series of Facebook status updates I made, that I often use words with meanings not everyone knows, like *quotidian, gravid, somnolent,* and *plangent*. I don't use them because they sound important or fancy; I use them because they are an inherent part of my lexicon—the vocabulary of a person, language, or branch of knowledge—and they made their way into common usage in my speech and writing. Plus, I like the way they sound. As an only child, my primary form of entertainment was reading, which has carried over into my adulthood. (Reading widely is a wonderful way to stretch your vocabulary, by the way.) I soon came to realize that these words were part of my written voice, that they emerge regularly (and sometimes need to be pared back from excess usage), and that even when I try to curb them they show up. They're just a part of my lexicon.

You, too, have a lexicon, whether you know it or not. Some writers' voices are colored by their geography. Southern writers often have a noticeable voice that's drawn as much from the literal sound of the Southern accent as from the rich physical geography and powerful history; writers who speak multiple languages often bring their first language over into English. Writers who grew up among highly intellectual people may write differently from writers who grew up among those who never graduated high school. And trying to force yourself into another person's "voice" is not only nearly impossible—unless you're an expert mimic—it's tantamount to tossing away your own style and individuality. Better to learn to become aware of and familiar with the language you use. If you feel you'd like to stretch your vocabulary, there are easy ways to do this, but instead I recommend getting to know yours as though it's a language you're learning for the first time.

Steer Clear of Conformity

In chapter two I asked, "What are you willing to risk as a writer to go for your goals, to drum up your dreams?" It's a question only you can answer and one that may take some meditation time. But inside the answer is a map that will lead you toward authenticity if you let it. Once you know what you're willing to risk, you will be more inclined to make choices that align with what feels right for you. Your Writer's Code is the foundation of your authenticity. Once it's in place, you have a plan you can stick with, even when faced with the desire or demand to conform.

So now you're stumbling, running, or waltzing toward the discovery of your voice. Someone wants you to write something "a little more like this." Or perhaps he's asking, "Could you just change the theme of it?"

Can you? Will you?

You can. You might. But does it resound with the code you made for yourself? Do you really want others to dictate what you say and how you say it? I venture you're better off writing like you.

It's natural to look for support, encouragement, and help when things get hard; in fact, I recommended forming a Creative Support Team in the last chapter. But being your own ally means that:

- you trust yourself.
- you determine your own value.
- you advocate on your own behalf.
- you make your own writing practice.

- you decide what goals to pursue.
- you choose what feels right for you.

Being your own ally means that you stop looking outside yourself for validation and affirmation, and find it, generate it even, inside yourself first. I know that may sound a little easier said than done. I'll speak more extensively on this in chapter eight, "Go Where You Are Welcome."

WORK IT

1. When you meet with resistance in your writing or feel uncertain about whether you're writing something true to you, ask, *How am I being vulnerable here? What is another way I can express this authenticity where I may either be heard or gain the skills or connections I need?*

2. Comb through your less-formal writing, the writing no one will see—journals, letters, notes for stories—and highlight phrases that stand out and words you use often. Become familiar with your own lexicon and learn to polish and be proud of it.

3. Now go through your more formal work: the stories, novels, and essays written with the idea of publication or feedback. Notice recurring themes, happenings, and characters. Do you return often to favorite settings? What scenarios, moods, and tones show up over and over? Make a list and watch your unique voice emerge.

MOVE IT

We all have different bodies that move in different ways and are comfortable with different kinds of exercise. What we all have in common is a need to take breaks from extended periods of sitting and writing. Whether you love slow stretching or hard cardio, pick from one of the following exercises for your five-minute stretch break.

A quick Google or YouTube search will show you how to do any of the following. If you have injuries, please be careful and cautious, or consult your doctor.

- **LOW INTENSITY:** Gentle neck and head stretches. First tilt your head to the right, toward your shoulder, and use your right hand to pull your head just a little further to the right. Do *not* stretch to the point of pain. Repeat on the left side. Next, interlace your fingers, and if you can do so without pain, reach your arms behind your head, palms facing the back of your head, against the base of your skull. Press your head back toward your hands, while your hands resist the pressure slightly. You can also tilt your head toward your chest and then alternate the move and look up at the ceiling.

- **MEDIUM INTENSITY:** Downward dog yoga pose. If you've ever seen a dog stretching, you'll know how this pose got its nickname. With palms on the floor, butt in the air, and feet flat on the ground, you make a sort of triangle of your body, pressing into your palms and soles, and stretching your spine upward. Hold the pose for as long as is comfortable, then push forward into child's pose (folded forward like a baby taking a nap). You can repeat the stretch a couple of times.

- **HIGH INTENSITY:** In one-minute intervals, do one of the following exercises two to three times, with ten seconds of rest between each one: jumping jacks, burpees, or mountain climbers.

chapter 4

TAME TIME

> *"The time you spend on art is the time it spends with you; there are no shortcuts, no crash courses, no fast tracks. Only the experience."*
>
> —JEANETTE WINTERSON, FROM THE ESSAY "THE SECRET LIFE OF US"

You know what they say about time: There's never enough of it. It's not on your side. It's elusive and wily and always seems just out of reach, especially if you live in the modern world with its copious responsibilities. Writers are always trying to find it, net it, and pin it down like a precious butterfly from a rare Amazon jungle.

I feel your pain, so I'll get the hard truth out of the way first: *Time is nonnegotiable in a writing practice.* You need it; your writing practice needs it. Without time, you have neither writing nor practice. As much as I like to believe that time is "just a concept," if you choose to ignore it, deadlines won't get met and stories won't get written.

Here's the good news: You have more time than you think. But first you need to get some things out of the way.

CARVE OUT DISTRACTIONS

I love what Julia Cameron says about distractions: "It is a paradox that by emptying our lives of distractions we are actually filling the well." It often seems like doing "more" will lead to greater productivity. But this is not the case. I'll never forget the relief I felt when I read the National Public Radio (NPR) story that disproved multitasking as an effective means for getting multiple things done at once. "People can't multitask very well, and when people say they can, they're deluding themselves," said neuroscientist Earl Miller. "The brain is very good at deluding itself."

What brains can do, he said, is shift focus from one thing to the next with astonishing speed, which makes you think you're actually getting multiple things done at once—but you're not. Instead you're using what thought leader Linda Stone coined as "continuous partial attention." This means that you appear to be working on multiple things at once: reading an article and sending e-mail (or, more likely in this day and age, checking Facebook and texting someone), but you aren't doing any of those things with full attention. You're left with just as many tasks at the end of each day, only half-completed.

Many creative people attempt multitasking and plate piling. I used to be a master of taking on so many projects that I ran on adrenaline-fueled stress, and eventually I became addicted to stress endorphins. I couldn't get motivated until a tight deadline (or several) was upon me.

The things that distract you from your writing often give you a form of pleasure or a rush of endorphins. But these distractions also fritter away both time and mental energy for the writing you hope to do.

Most writers need focused quiet time to work (and if not quiet, definitely focused). I didn't realize how much I needed, as the old adage goes, until it vanished for nearly five years following the birth of my son. But even for those without children, time is so much easier to fill now—there are more methods than ever for distraction, a fact which only increases the amount of downtime you end up needing. You can enter a state *beyond* empty that I call "creative malnourishment," and it's dangerous to productivity.

Step one to creating more time to write is to carve away your distractions. Not all of them, and not all the time, but to start taking a look at where you spend "partial attention" on less important activities that could be reserved for "full attention" on your writing. These can include time spent on social media, a sudden desire to clean your house during writing time, taking phone calls, watching television, putting others' needs before your own, fixing your car, running errands, volunteering for events that will steal from writing time, and many more—all of which I'll discuss in chapter six, "Build Boundaries." We'll also talk about how to negotiate your commitments to your family, friends, and career in that chapter.

ORGANIZE YOURSELF

I'm going to wager that you fall into one of two main categories of organizational style: (1) You thrive on a kind of controlled chaos—your desk is a mess of papers and flotsam whose order only you understand—or (2) you need your work space to be neat and orderly so that your brain can follow suit. If you're interested in categorizing yourself further, these two organizational styles are often referred to as "right-brained" or "left-brained." There's a lot of information out there about what it means to be one or the other, but I find that taking quizzes to determine which type you are can become just another distraction.

It's important to know your style of organization, because you don't want to waste that precious writing time trying to force yourself into a method that doesn't work for you. I've spent countless hours implementing systems that seem to revolutionize the lives of other people, trying to organize, file, and label the constellation of papers that usually obscure the surface of my desk. And guess what? None of those systems ever lasts for me, because the only one that works is to stack the papers of the relevant projects on top of my desk where I can see them and find them at a moment's notice. For those of us from the "controlled chaos" school, organizing can become another distraction from actually getting down to the writing.

On the other hand, if you *are* a person who needs the kind of order that allows for a clean desk, you know it. You knew it when you read the above paragraph and shook your head in horror at the thought of a desk run rampant with papers, books, and various writing utensils. Your task, then, is to separate your organization time from your writing time so that you can, in fact, let yourself write when the urge is upon you rather than file folders or vacuum your office.

No matter which way your brain swings, consider the conditions under which you best write successfully.

- Quiet office? Noisy café with background noise?
- In the presence of other writers, or alone?
- In the morning, afternoon, or evening?
- On a full stomach, or empty?
- With or without caffeine?
- In short bursts or long stretches?
- In between work, or in a dedicated writing session?

The sum of these answers is, of course, your ideal conditions for writing. You won't always get your ideal conditions, but you will *be aware* of them, and that is a big step toward carving out the time you need to get the writing done.

Now ask yourself: "How much writing do I need to do to feel accomplished?"

The "pat yourself on the back for hard work" phase comes at different stages for every writer. Before I had a child, I was a "rise at 5:30 A.M. and write for two hours every morning" type of writer, in which I could pump out about 5,000 words in a sitting. Anything less than that and I didn't feel I'd done enough. Since my son's birth in 2008, I give myself great accolades if I just make *any* time to write in a day, and sometimes I have to bring that standard down to "in the week."

It's important to have a baseline. A great baseline is "some" writing every day. If you can set up your writing practice to allow for a lot of writing, good for you, but every bit of time you make for writing counts and makes a dent.

One way to keep track of your baseline goals is to create a simple table in Excel or Word and print it out. Let's say your baseline is to write 2,000 words every day. You can create a simple table that you check off for each day you write. You can even reward yourself for hitting or exceeding your baseline goal: Maybe you wrote 2,000 words every day for a week, which earns you a date night with your spouse.

BASELINE GOAL	COMPLETED?	TOTAL DAILY WORD COUNT
Monday: 2,000 words	✔	2,000
Tuesday: 2,000 words	✔	4,500
Wednesday: 2,000 words	✔	2,000
Thursday: 2,000 words	✔	5,000
Friday: 2,000 words	✔	2,400
Saturday: 2,000 words		
TOTAL WORD COUNT		
GOAL REACHED? REWARD:		

BREAK MENTAL BLOCKS

I'll be addressing the subject of mental blocks from various angles throughout the book, but I want to make a note in this chapter that it's okay if you experience a block for taming time. Even if your burning desire is to write every day, and, more specifically, to seek publication, when it comes to really doing what this chapter asks—carving out distractions and determining the right conditions for your successful writing practice—you may find yourself resisting. Resistance is a form of fear. Your fears may run the gamut, but there's no doubt that making time equals taking your writing practice seriously, and with seriousness comes commitment and responsibility. Or as Steven Pressfield, author of *The War of Art*, puts it, "The more scared we are of a work or calling, the more sure we can be that we have to do it."

It's okay to be a little afraid and do it anyway. Sometimes fear is just a sign that you are embarking on an important path.

PREVENT PROCRASTINATION

Don't worry; I'm not here to shame you about any efforts at putting off your writing. We all do it—procrastination is as natural to any kind of work as is the need for reward. I believe that most of you procrastinate not so much because you're afraid or that you require pressure to get working but because of Newton's law: "An object at rest stays at rest."

If you don't put the writing first, you inevitably put your energies elsewhere, and the ball starts rolling down one of a variety of slopes having nothing to do with your writing. You can use therapy or church to help you figure out why, but for our purposes the reason is not so important. When you put your writing first—whether that means rising before work or before your children wake up, or before you check e-mail or pay bills—you are statistically more likely to write and keep writing. At the end of this chapter, I've included a list of great apps designed to help keep you focused on your writing.

If you're an evening writer, obviously you won't be up and writing at the start of the day, but you still want to approach whatever writing time you designate as a kind of sacred space (more on that in chapter six, "Build Boundaries") and not place another distraction or task ahead of it.

Procrastination is also often a sign that you are resisting something in particular because of feelings it elicits. Humans are odd animals; we sometimes resist the very things we love or desire out of a fear of failure or a fear of commitment. Authors David Bayles and Ted Orland, in their wonderful book *Art & Fear*, describe this conundrum as "a species of fear—that fear that your fate is in your own hands, but that your hands are weak."

Make this your mantra: *I put my writing first.*

USE WAITING TIME TO WORK

We can't talk about time without talking about waiting; if you put your work out in the world seeking publication or feedback, rarely does anyone answer immediately, even with the digital speed of life.

Nearly nothing is as pleasurable in a writer's life as the moment of fulfillment, that warm buoyancy of completion, validation, or approval. As a writer, these moments are unpredictable, on a time line all their own. Maybe you've experienced the fulfillment of having finished a draft or met a deadline. At its apex is the fulfillment of validation: Someone loves or wants to publish what you've written. In that moment, all you know is that at the top of the steep climb of your hard work, fulfillment is the mother of all endorphin rushes—it's like a runner's high meeting unconditional love and manifesting in the biggest pat on the back you've ever received.

Waiting for feedback, on the other hand, can often feel buzzy and uncomfortable. It's an anxious tilting toward the future that promises to bring ... well, that's just the question, isn't it? When you wait, you enter the shroud of the unknown. Inside waiting, it's things-go-bump-in-the-night dark. You might even lean toward despair before you know the outcome. You wonder what is coming next, if you deserve to have it, if you really want it, if you are ready to take the risk. Most writers I know are sensitive people. You might let the waiting become too heavy, too much. You might let it push you toward despair.

Ideally you will learn to enjoy waiting, at best, and to treat it as an exercise in trust, at worst. As writers, without trusting the outcome of your work, you're all too susceptible to doubt and despair.

Why?

Because after fulfillment and acceptance, what comes next? Eventually the blush fades, the high recedes, and you are back to writing. At the end of the day all that matters is loving the work. The work is all you have. Sometimes it leads to validation and publication; sometimes it leads to a deep feeling of inner satisfaction.

You must train yourself to use the waiting time as work time so you won't waste that time worrying, lamenting, or stressing. If you're submitting stories to magazines or queries to agents, keep the cycle going. Submit, work. Submit, work.

Keep producing, gnashing, stretching, refining, testing, polishing, and most of all: persisting.

DEALING WITH "TOO MUCH TIME"

I know, I know, saying you have "too much time" is like saying you have "too much money" or that your car is "too new." If this is a problem of yours, not many will sympathize. But it absolutely can become a roadblock to writing if you are prone to procrastination or distraction. When I quit my last "real job" a decade ago, on my first work-at-home day I sat in front of my computer and stared at it nervously as if I were on a blind date. I had freelance articles, editing jobs, and fiction all waiting for me, but I could attend to none of them. For a brief time, without a boss, a schedule, or a deadline, I floundered: I got up and dug in my garden, made lunch, took a walk, and finally, right at the end of the day, just before my husband came home, I plowed into the work.

Only to run out of time.

It took me several weeks to strike up a good working rhythm. If you are one of those lucky people who has too much time, try to see it as a blessing and not a curse. But keep in mind that your projects won't magically organize themselves. Your writing won't threaten you with punishment for not doing it. Only you can hold you accountable. Try prioritizing as follows.

1. Put your writing first.
2. Work on what's due the soonest (a deadline, a commitment to a critique partner).
3. Then work on that which you most want off your plate.

At the end of the day, you have exactly as much time as you allow yourself. I know mothers of five who've squeezed writing into two-hour nap sessions for years, writers with full-time and more-than-full-time jobs who've written novels on their lunch breaks, and writers who rise before the sun does or long after the family has tumbled into slumber. The time is there, waiting for you to dig it up like a long-buried treasure.

WORK IT

1. Make a list of all the "possible" time slots in your day that you could devote to writing but aren't. Or make a list of the distractions you have in place that could be pushed aside to make way for writing. Ignore the voices that say, "It's too hard" or "It won't happen." Now look at your list and pick two time slots in which you can write or two distractions you can replace with writing time.

2. Select from one of these fantastic apps that don't allow you to access the Internet within set times or only allow access within certain parameters (such as allowing you to only access certain sites). This will prevent the temptation to go online to peruse your Twitter feed or a friend's blog when you've committed to writing.

- **ANTI-SOCIAL** (anti-social.cc): prohibits access to distracting sites within timed blocks.
- **SELFCONTROL** (selfcontrolapp.com): a free, open-source Mac application that lets you add sites to a blacklist so you can't access them.
- **WRITE OR DIE** (writeordie.com): an app that times your writing progress and allows you to set word goals. It's equipped with "reward" and "consequence" modes: In reward mode, the app "rewards" you with pleasant images and sounds after you hit a certain word count. In consequence mode, if you sit idly without typing for too long, the screen turns red, and unpleasant noises begin to play.
- **STAYFOCUSD** (bit.ly/1C1JGyP): a customizable app that limits the time spent on time-wasting websites.
- **WRITEROOM** (www.hogbaysoftware.com/products/writeroom): an app for Mac users that serves as an alternative to Microsoft Word. It's a full-screen writing environment that eliminates the clutter of word-processing programs and allows for distraction-free writing.

MOVE IT

When you take a break to stretch, the most overlooked parts of your body are those that probably do the most work: your hands! Pick one or several of the following exercises for your stretch break.

- Squeeze a tennis ball in one hand, slowly compressing the ball as far as you can go and then releasing. Do this five to ten times with each hand.
- Lace your fingers together, and then press your palms facing out and away from you. Straighten your arms until you get a nice stretch.
- Go into active child's pose: Fold your knees under you and bend forward with your head toward the floor. Instead of planting your arms and palms flat, dig your fingers into the ground like claws, pressing them into the earth. This strengthens fingers and stretches arm muscles. (If you need more help with this pose, do a YouTube search for a demonstration.)

chapter 5

FIND BALANCE, BE PRODUCTIVE

"If we attend continually and promptly to the little that we can do, we shall ere long be surprised to find how little remains that we cannot do."
—SAMUEL BUTLER, FROM *THE NOTE-BOOKS OF SAMUEL BUTLER*

Surely you know one or more prolific writers who produce so much material that you wish you could bottle their energy and drink it down later for yourself. You may picture them at their desks, typing away, with papers stacked manuscript-high beside them. (And maybe it's only me, but I always imagine these productive writers sitting before old-fashioned typewriters. That's how romantic and fantastic the notion is in my head.) Perhaps you even feel a little envious or resentful of their output: *Hey, that could be me if only I didn't have to [fill in the blank].* It's easy to believe that a large quantity of writing is a sign of productivity, and thus, if you are not writing reams yourself, you aren't being productive. But more writing does not necessarily equal better-quality writing, nor does faster writing lead to faster achievement of your goals. This chapter will help you redefine what productivity means and looks like for you.

CONSIDER THE PROS AND CONS OF FAST DRAFTING

For at least six years, I, like millions of other slightly crazed, well-intentioned writers, have participated in NaNoWriMo—National Novel Writing Month—in which writers attempt to produce a 50,000-word novel in thirty days while running on caffeine, blind faith, and a spirit of adventure. The part of my mind that is like an endurance athlete (trust me, it's a very small, short-lived part) always thinks this sounds like a great idea and enjoys the endorphin rush of writing toward a fast finish. And it is fun at various stages—particularly at the beginning before reality has set in. But you know what the honest truth is? It kills me every year. By the end of November I am the crankiest, most burned-out, and spent writer I know. I can't bear to look at what I've written, my head hurts, I've snapped at my family more times than I can count, and I usually celebrate my finish with a big, fat head cold.

I'm not saying not to do NaNoWriMo—in fact, on the contrary, I think every writer should do it at least once to experience what a true writing marathon feels like and find out how much work goes into being that deeply engaged in your writing. However, just because you write something fast doesn't mean it will be complete and publishable when you reach the "finish line." In fact, I've found I usually need an additional six months to a year after writing these fast drafts to make any sense of them and another similar stretch of time to revise them. A fast draft gets it down—yes, *hallelujah! Amen!*—but it doesn't finish it for you.

So if you are going to undertake fast drafting (and there are even more radical versions than NaNoWriMo: the two-week official version of "Fast Draft" and the "write your novel in a weekend" boot camp style), be prepared to come out of those sessions with a lot of work left to do. Accept that what you write quickly may need more revision later. And don't beat yourself up because you didn't write a fully finished masterpiece in thirty days or less; great works aren't written in one sitting. Consider, too, that you may need a lot of downtime after the intensity of the process—and that's time away from your writing, which might ultimately be counterproductive to your overall output.

SET MANAGEABLE INTENTIONS AND GOALS

All of this brings me to a very important topic for making yourself productive in a balanced way: intentions. When I teach plot and scene to my writing students and clients, I stress the importance of characters having smaller intentions in every scene and larger dramatic goals to move the story along. A character without intentions wanders around her narrative. A plot without goals is a series of interesting but disconnected vignettes.

The same is true for your writing life. Intentions are daily motivators in small, manageable pieces; they spur you into action and carry out your tasks on the way to your goals. Your goals are the big-picture items—to be a published author, to have that story you wrote accepted by *The New Yorker*, to query literary agents—built from the efforts of your intentions. The more intentions you create for yourself, the more likely you are to follow through. In fact, Dr. Gail Matthews, a psychology professor at Dominican University in California, did a study on goal setting with 267 participants that found that people are 42 percent more likely to achieve goals just by writing them down. Perhaps the very act of committing important intentions to the page puts them at the forefront of your mind. Writers know better than anyone the power of putting a thought to paper—it makes the item more real, focuses your attention, and motivates you to take action. Or as Henriette Klauser, author of the wonderful *Write It Down, Make It Happen*, says, "Life is a narrative that you have a hand in writing."

Don't Make To-Do Lists

From here on out, I'd like you to stop making to-do lists. Nothing causes more anxiety than a list of items looming like a dictator with instructions to *do*! You can all but feel a whip being cracked at your rear, can't you? Instead, set yourself up with daily intentions as I mentioned above. Intentions are a kinder, gentler way to nudge yourself along. In fact, I recommend that you make a master list of action items for the week or month, and keep it in a binder. Each day choose only the most crucial items from the master list and write them on an erasable whiteboard, which will then serve as your daily intentions list. I do believe in creating parameters for your writing so that you are less likely to sit at your desk panicking in front of the blank page because you don't know where to start. Just don't create so many parameters that you stymie yourself.

Some examples of the kinds of intentions you can set for a writing session are:

- to outline a scene.
- to write a specific number of words.
- to write a piece to a specific theme or for a specific publication goal (a contest, a writing prompt).
- to finish a nonwriting-related project that is keeping you from your writing.
- to pick up a scene or story where you left off last time.

Try to *avoid* putting items like this on your daily intentions list.

- Finish my novel.
- Write one hundred pages.
- Plot out a new seven-book series today.

Part of being a creative person means that you may be more sensitive and open to ideas, energies, people, stories, and so on than most. That means you have to learn to corral and guard your writing time so that you use it wisely, like a precious elixir. It also means that you need to be careful not to set yourself up for failure by heaping more on your plate than you are liable to do or capable of completing. It means learning that voracious and prolific writing does not equal success. In fact, writers can be prone to "hypergraphia," a condition of producing excessive amounts of writing. It's related to temporal lobe changes in the brain consistent with hypomania.

Set Long-Term Writing Goals

It may seem a little late in the book to have you start thinking about long-term goals for your writing practice—except that I know you've been thinking about them all along. You were likely thinking about them when you picked up this book, and it's partly why you did pick up this book.

Now I want you to reconsider your long-term goals. If you have one big, intimidating goal, such as "get published by Random House," that's fine, but what does it really mean? In other words, you need to consider the steps that will make your goal possible. If your goal comprises a series of many smaller intentions along the way, then you might begin to look at it as doable. Goals that maybe once seemed out of reach become possible: A novel is written, after all, in a series of small, manageable scenes and chapters, not necessarily in a month. Or, likewise, you may realize that the steps involved in trying to get *The New Yorker* to publish your short story are not as worth your while at this stage as seeking publication in journals more friendly to newer, less well-known writers. You might instead set an intention to publish many small pieces in smaller journals until you are ready to try your hand at the big guns.

Remind yourself that books are written sentence by sentence, not in complete chapters. Don't query an agent before a manuscript is complete; hark back to the discussion about logical next steps, and find the one that you are ready to take next, without jumping to the finish line before you're done.

WORK IT

1. Buy yourself an erasable whiteboard on which you can write your daily intentions. Don't keep a long list of all your intentions in an overwhelming list in front of you. (You may have a master list you keep in a notebook, but hide it away.) Every day, erase yesterday's intentions and copy only intentions from your master list that you can do that day. Try not to overachieve; instead strive to accomplish tasks in manageable chunks. Try to include "writing" on your daily intentions list every day, and remember to start with the most pressing task (anything that is deadline driven or that is driving you crazy) to get it out of the way.

2. Which of your goals seems more in reach after reading this chapter? Break down this goal into a series of smaller intentions or just the intentions you will set for your next session. What goals do you have that now seem worth pushing off to a later date?

MOVE IT

What's your "usual" comfortable stretch break? Ten sit-ups? A lap around the block? Set a goal to do just a little more during today's stretch break, whatever it may entail. Another minute, another repetition. Not twenty more reps, not an hour longer of exercise—*just a little more*. It's good to increase the amount slowly over time.

chapter 6

BUILD BOUNDARIES

> *"Time is the coin of your life. You spend it. Do not allow others to spend it for you."*
> —CARL SANDBURG

Writing is such a silent, solitary endeavor that many people in your life may not even know that you write at all, much less how often or how much time and effort you devote to your craft. Even those with the best intentions may not understand that the long stretches of time you spend staring out the window are not "interruptible" but rather crucial artistic musings. Those who read your work may assume you churn out every piece in one sitting, with no clue as to the number of hours, the agony, and the investment you devote to even the shortest essay. As such, you can't rely on people in your life, be they best friends or colleagues, to know how precious your writing time and energies are. *That's on you.*

A big part of building a lasting writing practice means not negotiating your writing time out of obligations, guilt, fear, friendship, or other reasons. It means talking about your writing as the powerful, purposeful, entertaining, beneficial work that it is. It's easy to tell yourself it's frivolous and inconsequential, particularly if it doesn't yet produce an income or attract readers, but that is the lie of the ego, which does not have your best interests at heart.

Remember your Writer's Code? That's more than a promise to your-self; it's a contract—a binding contract you will regret breaking. But don't despair: Your writing practice is a changeable, fluid creature. It ebbs and flows, squeezes down to the size of a pea, and then expands to fill multiple universes. A writing practice is ongoing as long as you always keep a part of yourself invested in it, give it just enough water to stay alive during the difficult times, and tend it into hearty fruition at the best of times.

It's easy to be swept up in the instant gratification of our entertainment culture. Everything's on demand, which makes writers feel that they must be, too. Many authors turn out a book a month to please serial readers, while others bust tail to put out a book a year to keep their publishers happy. I'd rather you look for inspiration from writers like Donna Tartt, author of *The Goldfinch* and two other novels, who produces one masterful, compelling book every eight to ten years. This is not to suggest that you must write at her pace but that you train your mind to see all your efforts as words that funnel into the larger body of your writing practice. The investment you make in time, practice, patience, and persistence will show in everything you do.

And really, let's put this into perspective: At the end of your life, do you think you'll be happier that you worked more hours at your day job, listened to someone else's advice for your writing, read someone else's manuscript, or frittered away time online … or that you gave yourself more time and energy to write? Yes, it's a rhetorical question, but the point is that it's easy to get lost in the day-to-day pressures of life.

CREATE A DO-NOT-DISTURB ZONE

Chapter four gave you strategies to carve out and commit more time to your writing. But once you carve it out, you need to learn to *protect* it. Your writing time is work time, and it counts. A writer I knew used to put up a "Writer Working" sign at her office door at home so that there was no question in the minds of her husband and children as to when she was in the do-not-disturb zone.

It's easy to tell yourself you can write and be available to your children, or that you can write while watching television, or that you'll get to it after you listen to your friend's woes (and, hey, all of those are legitimate activities). But harking back to our "object in motion" law of the last chapter, I guarantee that the "other" activity will quickly take precedence. Personally I find that my mind could easily become addicted to television, videos, YouTube, and Facebook. If I focus on one of those things, I won't easily pull away.

Show your family and friends (and, frankly, yourself) that you're serious by taking concrete steps to set up your writing space. Make your own "do not disturb" or "writer at work" sign, or tidy up that heap of old mail on your desk and hang up some art over it. Once you delineate the physical boundaries of your writing space, the energy boundaries will follow with ease. You can point your family to the clean desk or new sign and open a dialogue about when they can expect to find you working and how they can go about contacting you when you're in your zone.

Writing is an act of focused attention, and that doesn't come easily. I find that it takes a bit of restless motion—pacing my office, shuffling papers—and false starts before I really get "stuck into" the writing, a phrase I take from my friend Alegra. If you're only giving it the "continuous partial attention" I've written about, you're treating it the way my childhood best friend and I used to clean her room: by shoving all the toys and mess into the closet and under the bed, which is to say you're not really doing it at all.

BUILD ENERGY BOUNDARIES

Some people in your life add to your personal well of creative energy, while others steal it—intentionally or not. Do you know how to identify when someone is draining your personal well? If you feel tired, discouraged, negative, or depressed after spending time with that person, there's a good chance he or she is what I call an "energy sucker." Some of these people may be family members, co-workers you have to see on a regular basis, or long-time friends. I'm not here to advocate that you cut those people out of your life—but you should protect your writing energies from them. Writing energy is gossamer and fragile in its early stages. New ideas, fledgling courage, and burgeoning possibilities can be especially susceptible to energy suckers. These are not the people you want to share your early drafts or bold first steps with. Energy suckers will take the breath right out of your fledgling ideas and can even steal from your sense of value as a writer. You must learn to identify these people in your life and keep them separate until you and your writing are stronger. Think of them as germs that you must shield your newborn baby—your writing—from.

Until you're sure of a person's effect on your writing energies, don't chance having your energy distracted; stick to your Creative Support Team for company, sharing, and feedback.

LEARN TO SAY NO

Writers need each other, and most rely on each other for everything from feedback to cheerleading. If you keep at the writing game long enough, you will inevitably be called on to offer help, assistance, blurbs, critiques, referrals, and more to other writers. And if you're anything like me, you'll feel that it is your duty to say yes at every turn, both because you want to help and because you may need to call in favors of your own in the future. (In chapter seven, I'll talk about ways to successfully serve and give as a writer.)

Here's the thing: Eventually you need to say no. If you are madly writing and someone wants you to stop and read his manuscript, you may need to say no. Or just "not now." Interrupting your own rhythms doesn't serve your practice.

As author and research scientist Brenè Brown says, "Daring to set boundaries is about having the courage to love ourselves, even when we risk disappointing others."

Her point is that it's far better to disappoint someone for a good reason than it is to carry inevitable resentment, and lose time and energy, from having said yes. Your friend or colleague will get over her disappointment, but you'll carry the resentment for a long time. And resentment is counterproductive to creative energy.

Besides, saying yes to too many nonwriting projects is a form of both procrastination and self-sabotage that you just don't have time for.

PLUG ENERGY LEAKS

I could write an entire book on the ways we leak our creative energy, and those ways have little or nothing to do with people in our lives. In the end, you are always responsible for finding and patching these leaks inside yourself and for saying no and setting boundaries. Here are a few other ways you might be leaking creative energy.

- **MULTITASKING.** Remember, your brain can focus on one cognitive task at a time. You may believe you're doing three things, but you're actually doing three things halfheartedly and most likely will end up with three incomplete projects.
- **RESEARCHING.** If you need to research for a book or an essay, do it at a time that is not earmarked for writing. Research is a seductive way to procrastinate, too.
- **SOCIALIZING.** Making a "quick call" or shooting off "a quick e-mail" to have someone help you with your writing project generally leads to not writing. Answering the phone or the front door or saying hello to a friend across the café are also likely to lead to a loss of writing time. The only exception for socializing while writing is if you're texting a friend to say, "Stretch break" or "Meet me at the coffee shop for a writing date."
- **CLEANING YOUR HOUSE.** File any house-cleaning chores under "procrastinating" if they coincide with your writing time. Houses will always become messy again, and though I understand the "orderly house, orderly mind" concept, your writing time is nonnegotiable and not interchangeable with house-cleaning time.
- **ORGANIZING.** Similar to cleaning, save organizing for its own time slot.
- **MARTYRING.** Yes, I know this isn't a verb; bear with me. If you believe you are raising yourself to a noble position of suffering by putting off your writing for someone else, particularly an energy

sucker, I promise you it won't be worth it. Your suffering won't be noble, the writing will go undone, and the person you devoted your time and energy to will not appreciate it. The truth is, your noble martyr time will only last a brief while, and then it will give way to resentment and frustration and creative emptiness. If you use helping someone else or putting someone else's needs first as a justification for not writing, in truth you've helped no one. You didn't write, and you'll now be frustrated with the friend in need. Be especially careful of this dynamic with "energy suckers" who don't see your writing as important; the more you do for them at the expense of your own writing and energy, the more you are cheating yourself.

AVOID BINGE WRITING AND WORKAHOLISM

The last thing I ever want to do is discourage a writer from writing. I think most of you probably fall into the category of writers that need encouragement and motivation to write. But some of you will need to build better boundaries around … yourself. That is, you need to rescue yourself from habits that exhaust you and steal your energy: for instance, those of you who, once you allow yourself to write, don't stop. You may binge write, staying up at all hours of the night, losing sleep, running on caffeine and sugar for several days, and then inevitably crashing. That's not healthy. There's no need to buy into the stereotype of the wild or mad writer, particularly if you have a career, family, or other set of responsibilities. If you live in a cabin or are independently wealthy, or have been given carte blanche by those in your life to write all the time, then by all means, carry on. But in general, you can't sustain a writing practice by working until you burn out.

If you are binge writing, I daresay you're probably not carving out the time to write in a regular, healthy way. Instead you steal from your rest time, your family time, and your work time, and you end up paying the price. These are the kinds of things that get people to work against you, set up a false sense of persecution, and prevent your writing from being respected, all of which leads to a whole other set of complex issues.

The solution is to be honest with yourself about how you spend your time. Circle back to chapter four and carve away the distractions that aren't working for you, and commit to your writing in healthy, manageable sittings. You, your writing practice, and your loved ones will appreciate it.

WORK IT

Make a circular graph. (Don't worry, there's no math involved, I promise. I'm a writer, not a mathematician.) First, draw a big circle that fills up a full page. Then draw two more circles of decreasing size so that you have what looks like a rudimentary bull's-eye.

Fill in names of people closest to you, or with whom you have to interact frequently, in the various circles. Write the names of your Creative Support Team in the innermost circle. In the next ring, write the names of "safe people"—those who do not steal energy from your creative self. In the next ring, write the names of people who you might call unreliable—sometimes they steal time, sometimes they don't, so you aren't going to label them "safe." And finally, outside the circle, put those who steal your time, energy, or worse.

The point of this exercise isn't to shame anyone, and I certainly don't think you should share this with the people you've listed. But this chart will give you a good look at who supports and who detracts from your writing practice. It's a real examination of the people you need to keep further from your writing practice and those you know you can bring close. If you have made a date to write in the afternoon and an "unreli-able" or "uncertain" friend wants to pop in for an unscheduled visit, you may remind yourself that it's not a good idea.

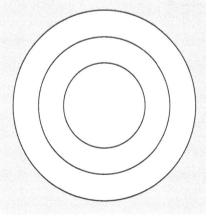

MOVE IT

Alegra is a fellow writer, one of my best friends, and a solid member of my Creative Support Team. She and I have had many discussions about what happens when energy-sucking people drain our vitality or when a bad feeling lodges inside us, brought on by one of the various travails of a writer's life. We've both discovered the magic in "releasing the stuckness" from our bodies through some sort of physical activity. Ironically, when your energies have been drained or stolen from a lack of boundaries, you need to replenish the body first before the mind will follow suit.

For the purposes of this chapter, in which you're taking a look at your energy leaks, we're going to do a replenishing exercise during your stretch break. This is basically a series of movements taken from yoga. But don't worry; you don't have to be a yogi to reap the benefits. Below is a graphic of the "sun salute" in yoga. Do these poses only in so far as you are comfortable. Don't push past comfort, and be sure to breathe as you go.

Illustration by Victoria Faye of Whit & Ware Design

chapter 7

SEEK TO SERVE

"No one is useless in this world who lightens the burdens of another."

—CHARLES DICKENS

After showing you how to carve out time, protect your boundaries, and say no more often, it may seem a little contradictory to offer ways to "serve" or mentor others with your writing. But I trust you'll come to find that serving or helping other writers is one of the most effective ways of fighting discouragement, despair, and the feelings that often keep us overly focused on the self.

Because writing is so much a part of you, it's easy to feel down and discouraged, and I aim to address this reality throughout the book. Sometimes you may just feel a kind of free-floating discouragement, whether you're a beginning writer trying to break in or an author from the trenches wishing to see greater success. It is in those downtimes, specifically, that this chapter will help you most.

There's one especially profound way you can "serve" other writers that won't steal from your time, cross your boundaries, or otherwise leak your creative energy: sitting down and writing. I know, I know, it's not new information. But let me say more.

SHARE YOUR STRUGGLES

Write about your difficulties, your fears, your anxieties. Share what's going on inside you. One of my favorite authors, Richard Bausch, offers up slivers of his process on Facebook to other writers. These are real, raw, deep expressions of what it's like to be a writer, and I (and thousands of others) find them deeply inspiring. He feels quite passionate about his purpose in writing, and he makes a wonderful point:

> Writing, if you have any gift for it at all, is something you are morally obligated to do as part of the social contract; there are people out there suffering the wounds and sorrows and terrors of existence who do not have the words to weather it, and it is the writer's place to give expression to that part of experience—to provide a sense of what Joseph Conrad called the "solidarity of the human family," and to give forth nothing less than the knowledge that no one, in the world of stories and of art, is ever totally alone.

You don't know when your words might touch, move, or help another person. You're only in control of producing them, polishing them, and putting them out into the world. You don't know who is waiting to hear exactly what you have to say or who will be affected by it. Just look at all the quotes gathered by authors on Goodreads: Most of these writers are not prophets, clergy members, or saints; they're just people writing about the highest and lowest points of human experience and sifting through the feelings in between. Often it's the times when you feel the lowest that you can best speak to others. And sometimes turning to your writing is a way to lift yourself out of that dark spot.

There are other powerful ways to reach people, and fiction is one such way. Of all the kind feedback I received from readers on my novel *Forged in Grace*, the most memorable appeared like a ghost in my inbox one morning. A woman named Sacha, who shares her name with a minor character that appears in my book, e-mailed to tell me she had lost her son, age twenty-one, to an accident. His name? Jordan Rosen-feld. (Did you get chills just now? Me, too.) My book is about a char-acter who discovers that her terrible burn wounds mask the power to heal. Sacha felt "spoken to" and "touched" by discovering her name *and* her son's in a book about healing. And it left me feeling touched, too, that a stranger would reach out and share her story of pain with me. Furthermore, this interaction was not something I could ever have anticipated in writing my book—it was a series of coincidences that stacked up to create a powerful moment of connection (or, dare I say, synchronicity).

One way to share your struggles as a writer is on your platform: your blog, Facebook author page, website, Twitter feed, and so on. Offer to have others guest-post on your blog on topics that support your vision, or you can link to their works. If you're active on social media, share the work of other writers whose words speak to you. Lift up your fel-low writers, and you'll feel yourself rising, too. You may also find that other writers would like to trade guest posts on their blogs with you, so that collectively you extend your reach to new audiences by sharing and taking turns with one another.

A Writer's Guide to Persistence is a manifestation of my own dis-couragement. I've been writing since I was eight and actively seeking a writing career since I was eighteen. And like any protagonist on a jour-ney, I've had epic setbacks along the way, dark nights of the soul, and feelings of terror that I was not strong enough to proceed on this path that is so very entwined with my heart. I found myself at a crossroads where doors felt closed and forward momentum waned. But I did as poet Rainier Maria Rilke asks young Mr. Kappus to do in his wonder-ful book *Letters to a Young Poet.*

> This most of all: ask yourself in the most silent hour of your night: must I write? Dig into yourself for a deep answer. And if this answer rings out in assent, if you meet this solemn question with a strong, simple "I must," then build your life

> in accordance with this necessity; your whole life, even into
> its humblest and most indifferent hour, must become a sign
> and witness to this impulse.

Rilke generously gave of his time and wisdom to the young Mr. Kappus, who needed a mentor. I'm quite sure it made a difference in that young writer's life, not to mention that it spawned a book that has gone on to inspire writers for decades since.

In asking myself the same question—"Must I write?"—I also found the answer to be yes. Sometimes the answer was, "Yes, but I don't know how or if I'll ever be published." Before long, one thing became glaringly clear to me: The urge to write would never go away, whether I saw big, flashy success or not. And in light of that truth, I realized I needed a way to push myself through my fallow periods, those times when either the muse was on vacation or rejections or criticisms had me facedown in the dirt.

I found it helpful to blog about my struggles. It was a bit like conducting my diary in public, but quickly I realized that people read and shared the posts that were real and raw but encouraging. If I shared about overcoming or continuing on the path despite my discouragement, it struck a chord in others. We all like to know we're not alone but also that others who suffer persist as well. I love to hear about the number of rejections famous authors racked up before they reached their goals or the years they put in before "overnight success" made an appearance. It reminds me that we're all here climbing this mountain together, just at different times and stages. And just like on an actual mountain, those above you have the power to pull you up. I've heard it said a hundred times in different ways that there is nothing better to illuminate the darkness than to help someone else by shining a light on your own struggles.

Even though you may never meet or have any live contact with your readers, writing creates a very real intimacy with others—if you're willing to reach out. Words open doorways and shimmy into tightly locked spaces in the minds and hearts of your readers, whether that reader is one person who stumbles upon your blog or thousands who buy your book. So the next time you find yourself fighting discouragement or writer's block, consider that there may be readers out there who need to hear what you have to say.

MENTOR ME

Several years ago a lovely young writer contacted me saying that she was new to a freelance writing career and would like to pick my brain. I didn't consider myself an expert, but I did have information about what had worked and failed for me as a freelance writer. We lived close enough that we met in person for coffee, and I downloaded every thought I could from my brain, shared contacts, and commiserated with the challenges she was already facing. I knew that I could have charged her money for the time spent giving her information or that she could have researched it online or simply learned the hard way, but I can't count the number of people who have helped me on my journey, who took chances on an unknown writer. It felt right to give back. She has gone on to be quite successful in her freelance career, and I take pride in having been a part of that. Most of all, it made me feel purposeful, useful, and helpful, all feelings I can call upon when I'm struggling otherwise. And I do believe that helpful energy always comes back to you in the end, often in ways you can't imagine.

If you're interested in mentoring, it isn't hard to find someone who needs it. I find mentoring within the online realm to be the easiest way to go about it. As a member of multiple Facebook writing groups, I find opportunities all the time to mentor others. You can do this, too, by searching Facebook with general terms like "writing groups" or more specific genre terms like "fantasy writers." You might also search for writing groups by your genre, your gender (women writers), or your skill level (newbie or professional writers). On an almost daily basis, a newbie writer pops into one of these groups brimming with questions.

If you're in a university or school setting, seek students who are in a lower grade or earlier stage than yours, or put up a notice offering yourself as a mentor. Most important, stay open; if you meet a writer, by chance or deliberate intention, who has questions you can answer, be ready to serve.

GIVE VOICE TO THE VOICELESS

Many of you are drawn to pen what haunts and fascinates you, which may involve stepping into the skins of characters who have vastly different experiences than you do. As Bausch says, many people in the world don't have the voice to express their suffering with the clarity or eloquence necessary to communicate their pain. Therefore writers are often the mouthpieces for the downtrodden, the underdogs, and the underserved. You might just be one of those writers.

Barbara Kingsolver started a literary award called The Bellwether Prize for Literature of Social Change to honor literature that probes into areas of important social issues and suppressed voices. Many, if not most, of the novels that have won the prize have offered a point of view rarely heard in literature. If you think you might be a writer who could speak for those who can't speak for themselves, you may find that in writing about them your work comes alive in powerful new ways as well as connects you to new audiences.

One of my favorite books that won this award is *The Girl Who Fell from the Sky* by Heidi Durrow. Her main character, Rachel, is a light-skinned, mixed-race child with a painful past who must live with her grandmother after her mother's death. Her grandmother's neighborhood is predominantly African-American, and she meets with much aggression because of her light skin. Yet in her mother's world, she was also rejected for being "too dark." The novel addresses important questions of race, identity, and mental illness, and offers a voice to the many mixed-race people in this country who don't feel at home anywhere.

Writing is a skill that many people need but don't possess. Since my son started kindergarten I've been called on more times than I can count to bring my skills to bear on behalf of his school projects. His first-grade teacher uses my weekly volunteer hour to have me walk the children through the construction of stories—the beginning, middle, and end—and teach them about revision, particularly that writers don't always produce perfect work the first time. It's a way to give my time and energy that benefits someone other than myself. It also makes my son associate positive feelings with writing, which makes me happy.

COLLABORATE

One of the most heartening aspects of the indie publishing movement is the willingness among indie authors to support and collaborate with one another. In lieu of mainstream publishing supports, these authors have taken it upon themselves to offer each other what they might need. In fact, author or writers' collectives and cooperatives have been trending upward in recent years. Writers with different skills pool resources and time and cross-promote to benefit each other to a larger degree than any of them could do alone. This is only one area where authors can collaborate in a way that serves both parties.

If you're unpublished, participating in a writers' critique group, whether in person or online, is a win-win situation. You give and get critique and possibly even moral support.

I've seen writers create anthologies to publish the work of authors they admire, and I've seen writers trading guest posts to promote each other's work.

I've even met writing "teams" in which two or more writers collectively produce a writing project together and then share the costs of publishing or the work of seeking to be published.

Whatever appeals to you, it's good to remember that the "loneliness" of the writing life need not be ever present. You'll find that many other writers are eager to connect and collaborate. And often collaboration produces creative ideas that might not have come to you alone.

At the very least I recommend that writers who are feeling stuck with a storyline or plot point "soundboard" with another writer; that is, bounce ideas off your writer friend to free your muse from the mire.

As Helen Keller said, "Alone we can do so little; together we can do so much."

WORK IT

What are some immediate ways you can use your writing to serve? Make a list in a notebook right now. Pick one way, and chop it into smaller goals. Say you'd like to host other writers on your blog; decide what themes and topics you're interested in and how often you'd like them to guest post. When you've made this decision, put out a request via social media, e-mail, and word of mouth.

Or you can make a list of advice you'd give to a burgeoning writer who is on a path similar to yours. What would you tell her? What mistakes have you made that she could avoid? Is there someone you know in real life who would benefit from your advice?

Lastly, consider writing a blog post or essay that you can share, or post about a lesson you learned the hard way, how you got through it, and what you would do differently if you knew then what you know now. Focus on how you felt, if and when you became discouraged, and what you did to pull yourself out of a tailspin.

MOVE IT

Here are a few fun ways to serve others while also serving your own need for a physical break.

- I'll bet you know at least one, if not many people who work and have a dog at home. Could you offer to take the dog for a jog or walk around the block a couple of times a week?

- Do you live near a local senior center? Almost all communities have one. The one attached to my gym is surprisingly busy, and every time I go there I see elderly folks using walkers and canes, in need of assistance through the heavy doors.
- If you are able-bodied, consider other kinds of places that are likely in need of a few minutes of your help. Does the library need someone to shelve books? Does the youth center need someone to shoot hoops with kids? There are tons of opportunities right in your own community.

PERSISTENCE IS PERSONAL
On Mentoring
By Charlotte Gullick, author of *By Way of Water*

I met Louis Owens in his Native American Novel course at the University of California Santa Cruz, where I took all of his classes and eventually began a novel in his creative writing course. This man—my first true mentor—believed in me. I struggled to pen a story about the people I come from: hardworking, religious, alcoholic, funny, rugged Westerners. For my senior thesis, I met with Louis each week, and every time I left his office, I knew I had work to do in order to breathe full life into the characters. Louis understood the importance of getting it right on the page, of weaving in complexity and vitality, and he guided me toward those qualities with a kind and knowing hand.

That first draft eventually became a novel that saw publication's light twenty days after my father's death and Louis's suicide. These deaths left me uprooted in a way that I still have trouble articulating. Dropped into the foreign landscape of grief, I struggled to find meaning, and I stopped writing for several years.

I threw myself into teaching, attempting to honor Louis's spirit. It was in the classroom that I found traction with my depression and with my writing, and all those students along the way have led me back to myself and the profound work of storytelling.

In particular, I am honored to work with Barry Maxwell, an older man coming to the surface of his life—sober—and claiming the disparate parts of himself he might have otherwise abandoned. He cares about language so deeply, and at the core of our mentor-mentee relationship is a sense that writing might just be the thing that saves us both, and that saving must be rooted in compassion, for ourselves first and foremost.

I think he is slowly allowing himself the title of writer, if only in small doses, perhaps overly aware of backslides and rude awakenings. In the first class with me at Austin Community College, he wrote:

> Beyond gathering enough cash for smokes and a buzz, my ambitions had evaporated, and I was resigned to ongoing futility. My life had become like a dying child in my arms, and I mourned as I bore it closer each night to the mass grave of the hopeless.

The image of his life as the cradled child blazed off the screen and into my heart. The fragility and the responsibility of our lives crystallized in this one line. It also helped me understand how Louis might have made his decision to end his life in a deep moment of disconnection and isolation, a heartbeat devoid of exactly these qualities.

As a mentor, I've grown more comfortable with anchoring other writers in their journeys. Together, Barry and I hold space for each other, maybe so that we might hold ourselves with a bit more care. Our touchstone conversations, on and off the page, underscore the power of connection to create meaningful work, and maybe, just maybe, to save lives.

chapter 8

GO WHERE YOU ARE WELCOME

"Signs may be but the sympathies of nature with man."
—CHARLOTTE BRONTË, FROM *JANE EYRE*

Here, nearly at the end of Part One, if you are still wondering what the right path is for you, let me reassure you: There are signs that will point you toward the kinds of writing, opportunities, and people that you should include in your creative practice. I borrow from the words of Story Waters, founder of the blog Limitlessness.com: "Go where you are welcome. You do not need to fight against things."

Have you ever found yourself working really, really hard to please someone, to earn approval, to receive attention or validation for your writing or your talent? And have you noticed that the harder you push, beg, or demand, the further away that validation or approval seems to go? This urge to "break into" or "bust through" the gates to get what you want can also tangle you up in a feeling of "I better hurry or there won't be enough left for me."

As a writer, you are probably prone to feeling pressured by the competition out there, as though you have to scramble to snatch up your success before someone else does. But if you refine your voice and vision and figure out what it is you have to say that no one else can in your particular way, no one will take your slot—because it exists only for you.

This is learning to live by what I call the "rule of welcome." This means that if you find yourself banging your proverbial head against a wall for a long time without results, if you're pushing too hard or feeling desperate, then it's time to take a step back—and possibly several steps around.

WHEN TO MOVE FORWARD

You will know the feeling of welcome—it's subtle, sometimes just the tiniest little tingle at the base of your spine that something is "right." The feeling shows up at times when you find that writing, submission opportunities, and inspiration flow effortlessly. For me this feeling of "rightness" has become a litmus test for whether an opportunity or idea is worth investing my time. And I'm not alone; a good friend of mine who grew tired of hearing "almost" and "not quite" about her novels from agents and publishers eventually opted to work with a hybrid publisher that did not require an agent. She didn't receive a big advance or huge distribution, but she did get to work with a team who helped put her much-labored-over novels into the world at last. It just felt right to her.

I believe in saying yes to as many new opportunities as possible (more on that in chapter thirteen, "Stretch Your Skills"), but I tend to pursue the ones that give me that sense of rightness. This is *not* to say that you will never have to work hard. On the contrary, welcome and work go hand in hand, but when the opportunity or idea is right, the work produces results as opposed to frustration and disappointment.

Don't beat your head against walls, literal and virtual, where you will not gain access. Stop seeking approval. Press pause on attempts to be as others think you should be or as you feel you should be in order to achieve.

Instead: *generate, create, deepen, practice, apprentice.*

Here's what I've noticed in my and others' writing careers: Doors pop open that would otherwise have been shut:

- when you are passionate about your ideas.

- when you commit to doing the writing no matter what.
- when you cultivate resilience and get back up after setbacks.
- when you do your research.
- when you seek out avenues that align with your work.
- when you make true connections with people.

When you feel the welcome sign—that buzzy little sense of certainty, familiarity, excitement, or rightness—it's time to take action. Even if what presents itself seems like the smaller or less glamorous opportunity, that welcome sign is important and will usher you toward what you need.

WHEN TO WALK AWAY

The harder part, of course, is admitting when the doors truly aren't opening after repeated and determined efforts. You need to learn to walk away from those doors and reevaluate. Ask yourself:

- Is it the avenue?
- Is it my work?
- Is it the timing?

Once it becomes clear that an avenue will not open, stop trying for a time and reassess. What you *can* control is devoting more creative energy to your work, doing more research, making connections, reading widely in the genre you write in. What you can't control is everything else: people's decisions, approval, or willingness to take a chance; timing; and who got there "first."

So don't waste your time lamenting the doors that haven't opened or never will. Instead, "Go where the energy welcomes you," as author Story Waters says. In other words, seek synchronicity.

SEEK SYNCHRONICITY

When you open yourself to synchronicity, you will begin to see a change in your writing practice. Renowned psychoanalyst Carl Jung coined the term *synchronicity* in his book *Synchronicity: An Acausal Connecting Principle*. Jung believed that life was not a sequence of random events but a reflection of a much larger, more elegant or "deeper" order. This deeper order led to the insights that people live within "an orderly framework" and are the focus of this framework. The realization of this, he said, was "more than just an intellectual exercise."

You might also see synchronicity as the phenomenon in which events line up in your life in such a way as to look like coincidence but feel like something much more meaningful. Say you've been toying with the idea for an essay about growing up with dyslexia, and then you go to see a movie that just happens to have a dyslexic character in it. It feels like a sign, doesn't it? Or maybe you're on a plane/in a café/at the gym and happen to start talking with this wonderful person who just happens to be a literary agent/magazine editor/fellow author. When you stay open and pay attention, synchronicity turns up everywhere.

No matter what you believe or think about the origins of life, we live in a world of beautiful patterns and unexplainable beauty. Our lives are like novels—we have such a short time to explore, discover, overcome obstacles, fight antagonists, make allies, and transform or discover our stories. What you do in your life can be empty and robotic, or it can be transformative, pushing you to new heights.

Since no one can argue for or against its existence, I advise you to see synchronicity in your writing life as a sign that you are moving into a place where you are welcome and that you are taking your writing life seriously and committing to your work. You may find synchronicity everywhere once you start looking for it: in conversations that lead to books that lead to new ideas that lead to blog posts that lead to writing projects that lead to new friends that lead to new resources that lead to Big Divine Inspirations.

Synchronicity is the way the muse speaks to you—it's one part your subconscious mind making connections that your conscious mind misses, thus urging you toward opportunities, and another part the language of patterns, a quantum physics of creativity at work. Synchronicity requires you to be open and present. You must look for it. You must not write things off as accidental. Turn off your logical brain for just a moment. Just as quantum physics cracks open the underpinnings of reality more boldly every day by revealing that there is far more going on in the big cosmic soup than we realized—that atoms can be both particle and wave, that the universe expands despite gravity's pull, that for all we know life is just a dream in a star's heart—words can be scribbled ink on a page or digital pixels or emotions plunged directly into a reader's heart.

Synchronicity requires attention on the part of the writer. I think it has a spirit of playfulness. It likes to make you giggle. It loves artists and writers of all stripes, because we are individuals who possess the ability to tap into its language.

Speak its language, my writing friends. Don't box yourself into a category or a container or a set of expectations. Writers often want an audience, but we wait for others to tell us we're worthy. We hope to squeeze through the tiny crack in the big gates on that hallowed road to fame and fortune, and squirrel away the words we should be sharing now.

There are other paths than just fame and fortune. *Many* others. Stay open. Write what you need to write, and share it with whom you want to share it.

Look for the synchronicity.

Allow the doors to fly open.

Do it now. Before your story is over.

WORK IT

I highly recommend you start a "synchronicity" notebook. You may call it whatever you wish: grand coincidences, goals that come to pass ... it doesn't matter how you frame it. Each day, record noteworthy events pertaining to your writing practice and goals. It could be something like "I picked up two books in a row today at the bookstore that shared the same name as my protagonist." Or "As I was working on an essay about my mother's death, I had this funny feeling to look through that box of old photos I've never opened; there I found a tiny diary she left behind that I never noticed or read before."

The more you track these events and situations, the stronger your lens will become to look for signs that you're moving in the right direction, and the more likely you will feel motivated rather than discouraged.

MOVE IT

So far, the "Move It" section has been largely exercise based. However, this chapter is about going where you feel good and happy. Today I want you to do something physical that aligns with this feeling of welcome or flow. Here are some activities and ways to loosen your body that might fall into this category. I'm going to ask you to leave your adult mind behind for this one, because some of the most joyful people on the planet are children, who aren't bound as much by our adult notions of being silly or weird.

- Dance or skip rope.
- Go for a swim, take a bubble bath or hot shower, or get in the hot tub if you have access.
- If you can, get a massage, a pedicure, a facial, or a mud bath.
- If you live in a snowy locale, get on a sled or ice skate.
- Place two tennis balls on the ground and roll your back across them.
- Buy a battery-operated massage tool and work out tense muscles.

The possibilities are endless, and you can vary any of these suggestions at any time.

PERSISTENCE IS PERSONAL
Like a Bach Duet
by Rebecca Lawton, author of *Junction, Utah*;
Steelies and Other Endangered Species; and other works

Many years ago I studied with a guitar teacher who liked to challenge his students with Bach duets. The music was full of arpeggios and scales that required full use of our fretboards. To help us increase our accuracy, we'd learn new economies of fingering that made grabbing notes easier. We'd set the metronome faster and faster, keeping up with the beats until we couldn't. Then our playing would explode into a series of wrong notes, and we'd laugh, take a deep breath, and begin again.

Some scale tones weren't reachable at the faster tempos, no matter how hard we practiced. When the pace was clearly beyond us, our teacher set it slower again. We found we could master all the music then, even the most demanding passages. "That's the point," he said. "You're learning the difference between what's difficult and what's impossible."

Writing challenges us the same way—not in speed necessarily but in range. There are the puzzles of research and language and sentence structure. There is simply mustering the energy to master our work. We may go, go, go until *bam!* We hit a wall.

Persistence in life is one key to success—falling down nine times and getting up ten. But persisting when there's no hope of success is a fruitless endeavor. It's admirable to keep trying in situations where satisfaction will be the ultimate prize, but it's only frustrating if we're only bloodying our noses and facing against a barrier again and again.

If you find that happening to you, stop. Rethink your approach. Take your work in a direction that does reward you.

You can decide to be like water, flowing where you're ultimately bound. Or like the streaming notes of a musical composition, you can carry on in liquid lines to the last measure.

How to tell the difference between the difficult and the impossible? Two ways, I think: *trust* and *practice*. Trust your gut sense of progress. You'll feel and hear your intuition saying, *This is right,* and then you can continue your life in that direction. Or, if you get information that says, *Wrong way*—a recurring situation, say, or an immovable attitude—you can change course. Life has other options. With practice, you'll recognize them.

It's the same on the page. Say you're stymied by a piece you're writing; it's just not working and you're out of ideas. You're tired; you've been at it three hours. You can push on, rewriting until you're defeated. Or you can give it a rest and return to it later with fresh eyes. When your mind and energy are clear, your beautiful gut sense will see the way through as it does with your life. The best parts will shimmer with vitality.

Most people I know have been in situations they've worked to improve, and some did get better. The situations that didn't improve were best left behind: unappreciative bosses, unsatisfying work, unyielding ceilings to progress. Those sorts of barriers are not so different from intractable prose: Sometimes we just have to work a little harder; sometimes we have to listen to our intuition telling us to push the reset button.

Trust your gut about what resonates and what does not. Know that you'll know what to cut and what to keep. Read and reread with your mind, heart, and intuition in tune with the work—at whatever speed allows you to really feel the energy. You will find the alive passages, and you can even choose to build on them. Those are the words you are meant to write; similarly, the life that flows is the one you're meant to live. Whatever the tenor of your life and work, you can retain the living, flowing, energized parts and ditch the dead.

Life and writing are like playing Bach duets. Knowing the difference between the difficult and the impossible takes hard work, practice, and wise respites. With intuition sharpened and in balance, you can always—*always*—enjoy the pleasure of good-natured laughter, take a deep breath, and start again.

chapter 9

PUSH THROUGH PERFECTIONISM

"Nobody's perfect. We're all just one step up from the beasts and one step down from the angels."
—JEANNETTE WALLS, FROM *HALF BROKE HORSES: A TRUE-LIFE NOVEL*

You hear the word *perfectionist* bandied about a lot, but what does it mean? Are you a perfectionist if you only show your best work? Are you a perfectionist if you hone and refine and polish your work? Are you a perfectionist if you commit all your free time to writing?

No.

Perfectionism—much like inertia, a force that strangles a person's ability to do any real writing—instills fears that you will never live up to a standard set in your mind or one that's been set for you by others. People in the throes of perfectionism have great ideas they often struggle to follow through on and small bodies of work they don't improve.

I don't believe that people are or are not perfectionists in a cut-and-dried way, but rather that some writers may be susceptible to and fall under the influence of perfectionism, a nasty intoxicant that brings very little actual pleasure. People in the grip of perfectionism are not lazy; they're afraid. And that fear leads to paralysis. If you think you might be in such a place, then be kind to yourself. (In fact, I venture that perfectionists are also great self-punishers—so please don't beat yourself up further if you realize you may be experiencing perfectionism.) The bravery, dedication, time, and vulnerability required of writers can be daunting. If you aren't at least a little bit afraid, it probably doesn't mean much to you to put your work out there.

It's not as simple as being a perfectionist or not—I see it more like an illness that overcomes you rather than a state of being. Think of it as a virus that may lie dormant inside you. You may only experience perfectionism in certain instances, when a particular fear gets the better of you; then you find yourself obsessing over a project or unable to let it go. In that case, you're simply having an *attack* of perfectionism, like a stomachache or the flu. And the cure for this condition is to keep writing.

COMMON FEARS TO OVERCOME

Let's unearth some of the most common fears at the root of perfectionism, those that keep you from letting go of your work or allowing others in to help you improve it. We'll first break down each of these fears so that you can free yourself from their grip, and then we'll go over strategies for combating them.

Fear of Failure

Failure is one of the most common reasons for paralysis among writers. There are so many opportunities for failure, from receiving a rejection letter to realizing that a work in progress isn't coming together the way you want it to. Every time I see a status update from a hardworking writer that says something like "How did I ever think I knew how to write?" or "My novel hates me!" I always think: *You're right on track—and that track is not failure.*

Creation is an act of chaos. I'm sorry to bring up the birth metaphor, but if you've ever seen a birth, human or animal, you know they are messy, wild affairs full of moaning and fluids and pain and frustration. Frankly, writing is not so different. The act of creation requires starts and stops, moving forward and back. Plenty of times you will write material that you will not use or pursue a path that proves to be fruitless.

But anything new is full of thrilling, marvelous wonder. No matter your spiritual point of view, if children popped out of the womb speaking French and completing times tables, you'd have to ask: What's the point? We create because it is full of wonder and awe, even though it hurts a lot, or at the very least causes grown adults to wander around in public muttering under their breath and eating themselves into donut comas. (No? Just me?)

Writing is a process of discovery.

You discover things about yourself, about your ideas and feelings. You enter into perspectives you may have always wondered about and deepen your exploration of those you've known intimately all your life. You try on lofty propositions. You escape, you revel, you get weird. (No? Can't just be me!)

Let me repeat: *Creation is an act of chaos.* And I don't mean uncontrollable, formless chaos but rather the raw, wild, bursting, daunting energies the universe is made of. Wild stuff. Atomic stuff. Fundamental stuff.

If you are experiencing any one of the million feelings of failure and frustration in the process of writing a book, I'm sorry to break it to you, but you are not failing. You are herding your own Big Bang into being; you are riding quantum possibilities.

When you feel the shivery feelings of failure coming on, remember:

- Everything you do for your writing practice deepens it. Fear of failure means you're doing something worthwhile and probably taking an important creative or personal risk necessary to growth.
- You really only fail if you quit (and even then, you can pick up and start again, so it's not true failure, either).

Fear of Being a Fraud

You might think that the fear of being revealed as a fraud would only strike those at the beginning of a writing practice: novice or newbie writers. Yet it seems to be a stock feeling that even the most successful writers carry. Even though you have published a story or a novel, have received an award or recognition, write every day for hours, are taking classes in writing, or have received a degree, sooner or later someone will lift that curtain and call you out for being full of it, a hack, an interloper. You may suffer from "imposter syndrome," in which seemingly successful people do not feel they deserve their success or that they will be revealed as imposters at any moment by their colleagues and others. This term was coined by Valerie Young, author of *The Secret Thoughts of Successful Women*, and publications such as *Forbes, Pacific Standard*, and *Slate* have run articles on the subject. Though men and women both experience it, women are statistically more likely to feel undeserving of their success than men.

This feeling of being a fraud or an imposter can only hold up in the face of proving something to someone else. As long as you seek to prove yourself, you're at the mercy, in essence, of that approval or praise. (More thoughts on the detrimental effects of praise in chapter sixteen.) Part of the necessary individuation of becoming a writer is learning to care less about what others think and more about achieving your vision as a writer. There does come a time and place for tailoring your work to an audience, but in so many cases writers stymie themselves at the wrong part of the process: as they're trying to get raw material onto the page. Those in the grip of perfectionism are especially prone to this; if you never get it down on paper, then no one can dislike it, right?

The fear of being a fraud also surfaces when you are given a chance to step outside your comfort zone. Someone or several people have decided you are, in fact, the very opposite of a fraud—they want to see your work, have you speak, or publish you. But suddenly you're crippled with terror that once they get what they've asked from you, they will be disappointed.

Over time, the more you do the work of a writing practice, the less fraudulent you will feel. It starts with your own acknowledgment that you are worthy and that you have something to say. With repetition comes confidence. The more you show up for yourself, the more you will trust yourself.

When you hear the lying voice of fraud in your mind, consider one of the following strategies.

- Give yourself permission *not* to show a particular draft or piece of work to anyone. Make yourself a deal. "I'll share the *next* draft." (Sometimes you just need to get past the fraud-crier in order to discover your project is better than you think.)
- Ask yourself these questions (I recommend journaling the answers): Who am I afraid of disappointing, and why? What will be the consequences of "failing" to deliver? Often you discover that your fear is amorphous—that when you look at the worst-case scenario, it's not nearly as bad as your anxiety is making you believe.

Fear of Having Nothing to Say or Being "Tapped Out"

You wrote a killer story, novel, or essay that knocked your professor, best friend, or fellow writer's socks off. They crowed, they raved, they promised you greatness would follow. Suddenly you're gripped by an icy sensation. What if that was it? Your one shot at glory—the best thing you are capable of producing? What if no more material comes again or will ever be as good? The panic rises into your gorge, and then you're hyperventilating on the floor in the fetal position, unable to write. Just me? No, I didn't think so. Like the fear of fraudulence, the fear of being a one-hit wonder is so common it should be a badge that you earn in the Writer Scouts.

Once I was the manager of a spa inside a health club. I was younger than most of my staff, and it was my first management position. But my boss liked me a lot, and amazingly, when we went to review my first-quarter sales goals for the products I was in charge of selling, I had exceeded them quite impressively (with no strategy in place). My boss gave me a bonus and words of praise, and then pointed out the ways we'd have to keep this success going. Within minutes, I was crying. My startled boss reared back and stared at me for a moment. "Are those tears of happiness?" he asked.

I shrugged, unable to explain my bizarre tears. All I could think the whole time we sat there, with my bonus check in my hand, looking at my boss's proud smile, was *How am I going to repeat this success? And if I don't, he'll know that I was never capable of it in the first place; it was a fluke.*

It's no different in the writing realm. You have a sudden success—a yes when you're used to hearing no—and the terror sets in. But it doesn't have to. Here are some tips for handling the fear of drying up.

- Give yourself this mantra (or one of your own): *Each project requires something different.* You don't have to bring the same skills or energy to every one. Just as parents find new love for each new child, you will find new energy and inspiration for all of your projects.
- Set a timer for ten minutes, and pick three random words out of the dictionary. Now write a short story, poem, or stream-of-consciousness freewrite that incorporates all three words. This exercise helps you generate new material from random prompts, which can alleviate the feeling that you'll never write again.

Fear of Being Out of Control

Nobody likes to feel as though they can't control the outcome of a situation or project. Even for the most "go with the flow" types, such feelings are challenging. Tossing your work into the world can feel precarious and unmooring, and, for many, that fear leads back to where this chapter started: perfectionism. Many a writer has clutched a beloved project to her chest for far longer than is necessary because the idea of letting it go feels a lot like letting go of control.

This can also extend to a fear of having *no* control over your work. If it's published, will you lose say in the editorial process? Will your voice be refined within an inch of its life? These are normal fears that, more often than not, don't bear out (though if you are really concerned, consider jumping straight to chapter twenty-three, "Go It Alone," about when and why to self-publish).

Creating art, putting it out there, and then awaiting feedback and publication can create immense anxiety. When you have nowhere to put your anxiety, it can lead to what psychologists call "binding anxiety"— behaviors that help a person cope with those uncomfortable feelings. These behaviors can range from revising a page over and over or never sharing your work, or, worst of all, a deep and complex "block" that feels as though it can never be broken. Try one of these strategies when you feel an overwhelming loss of control.

- Submit to publications or contests with deadlines. Pick writing contests as a way to force yourself out of holding on. Or ask a member of your Creative Support Team to set "deadlines" for you to turn over your work to them.
- Remind yourself that all works of writing are collaborative— between you and the reader. Even when you set out to create a specific vision, readers bring their own perceptions and opinions to bear. In a way, no artist is really in control of his or her work, because you can't control what people will think or feel while reading it.

Fear of Being Seen or Being Honest

At the root this fear is the fear of being rejected once the real, raw, honest truth is handed over to readers. Often we feel shame in putting our written words out there. Not only did you write your feelings into being, you now have hard, irrefutable proof in print that others can linger on, hold up, and assess you by. And that's scary. There's also the fact that your truth may be different from someone else's, so you open yourself to arguments, different opinions, and criticism. I think that's what makes the comments sections of many websites so appealing to some writers, because it offers the option of anonymity: They can say what they want and then go back and hide behind their screens, never having to face any of those people in real life if they don't want to— which is not always for the better.

But keep in mind the alternative: that you never express yourself, never improve upon your work, and keep all your thoughts and feelings bottled up.

When you feel that raw sting of potential rejection as you anticipate showing your real self in words, remember:

- For every person who might not like what you have to say, there is at minimum one, and probably many, who need to hear what you have to say and will be moved by it.
- Think of all the authors who have moved, touched, and inspired you. What if they had not put their work out there?

WORK IT

Choose the fear that resonates most strongly with you at the time of your writing. (You can also repeat this exercise for any other fear.) Make it the title or subject of a freewrite. For example, perhaps the fear of being a fraud is your chosen subject. Set a timer for a minimum of ten minutes and write a short story, a poem, or an essay without stopping to correct a thing. Just let it flow; don't stop to correct anything. Don't use quotation marks or punctuation, and don't cross anything out. Just start a new "sentence" when you feel stuck. This exercise helps transmute a negative feeling into a positive outcome—it's a mental version of the "Move It" exercises.

MOVE IT

Perfectionism needs an antidote in order to dissipate: sloppiness, looseness, or, more specifically, permission to let go. I highly recommend these exercises.

1. **DANCE SESSION.** Put on music, be alone, and get silly: head-tilted-back, limb-flailing, singing-in-the-shower crazy.

2. **RUN IT OUT.** If dancing it out is too much for you, try running it out. Run in circles, run up and down some stairs, even run in place. The endorphins of some quick cardio have a powerful way of jolting perfectionism out of your body.

3. **FINGER PAINT.** There's just something about finger painting that perfectly embodies what it means to let go of perfection. Try making a perfectly straight line with all that gooey paint on your fingers. You can't! It's a tactile experience of allowing yourself to loosen up a negative feeling and transform it through another medium.

Part Two
POLISH

chapter 10

BREAK THE BLOCKS TO CREATIVE FLOW

"If you tell yourself you are going to be at your desk tomorrow, you are by that declaration asking your unconscious to prepare the material. ... Count on me, you are saying to a few forces below: I will be there to write."
—NORMAN MAILER

There is nothing as heady as the initial spark of an idea that flows into a rush of pure inspiration—it's a feeling both holy and euphoric. Who wouldn't be addicted to the thrill of writerly gush? But like all things, eventually that gush becomes a trickle and possibly even stops. If you're like me, that happens about two-thirds of the way through a project. I make it over the great muddle of the middle and then find myself stranded on the path, wondering if I can go on.

And as exhilarating as inspired flow can be, it's opposite, writer's "block," is incredibly demoralizing, even when it means different things to different people. Some of you may struggle to find inspiration or to finish work that's been hanging in limbo for a long time. You may think you don't have anything to say (go back and visit chapter three, "Awaken Your Authenticity"), or you may struggle with procrastination (visit chapter four, "Tame Time"). But most of all, I find that creative block comes down to one of several elements I'll explore within this chapter.

COMBAT INERTIA

Rather than calling it writer's block, I like to think of the state of being unable to produce material as *inertia*: a powerful force that keeps you from doing your work. I argue that inertia actually serves a purpose: to give you something to work against and to force you to set or shift goals, plunge deeper into the writing, or let something go. For something happens—dare I say "magic"?—when you focus your attention on overcoming an obstacle: Your work begins to move, grow, and expand, and has a much greater chance at success.

While I am more than familiar with inertia now, at age forty, I *rarely* experienced it in my twenties and only a few times in my thirties. Then I had a baby at age thirty-three. Before, I could always force myself to write when I wanted or needed to, but after my son's birth and during the exhausting months of caring for a newborn, I became intimately acquainted with inertia—not only in my physical body, which habitually collapsed onto the nearest piece of furniture whenever possible, but mentally as well. My mind also caved inward and away from work: Returning to the keyboard or the page seemed unbearably hard, an act I might never undertake again because I'd fallen so out of practice. Once inertia strikes with its powerful gravity, it's incredibly difficult to pull yourself free again. It's easy to consider writing, much less the pursuit of publishing, an exercise in futility. You lay your weary muse in the road, and the vultures begin to circle, taking her for dead.

But she's not dead. *You're* not dead. There's life in you, and your project, yet. But now you will have to provide yourself with the momentum formerly granted to you by the tailwinds of inspiration, deadline, or competition. This effort against inertia may come as a big adrenalized burst—forcing yourself into a day of writing—or it might be slow and steady progress, bits here and there.

It's hard to remember that your great ideas won't birth themselves. They may appear to you of their own mysterious volition, but they require you to finish the process of creation. If you find yourself stuck in the glue of inertia, it's time to take advantage of one or more of the following strategies.

Assess Your Stage

The way I see it, there are only six main stages in writing and finishing a project. (Please understand that "revising" is often a stage that involves multiple drafts, but for the purposes of this chapter, I'll describe it as though it is one phase.)

1. Outlining and plotting
2. Writing the first draft
3. Seeking feedback
4. Revising
5. Proofing
6. Submitting to agents and/or editors, or self-publishing

Your block may stem from trying to do the work of a later stage when you haven't actually arrived at it yet. For instance, I know many writers who slow themselves down or even cut off their creative supply by trying to edit as they write. I always recommend refraining from revision during the drafting stage. Drafting is a wild process that requires room to roam and wander; if you try to crimp each thought right after you have it, you'll naturally stagnate.

Or you might find that your energy gets bound up in anxiety about the submitting stage. You worry about the competition, writing the perfect query, or how original your idea is—and the next thing you know, you've crimped off your creative stream. Be sure to take an honest look at the stage you're in before you trip yourself up by racing to a later one.

Make Writing a Priority

I know I've said it once, and trust me, I'll be saying it again and again, as often as I need to: You must make writing a priority. I know sometimes it seems hard, impossible even, to put writing first. But if you write first, before you do anything else, you'll carry that buoyant feeling around with you all day rather than the sludge of "I still haven't written." This doesn't necessarily mean to write "first thing in the morning" but at whatever time you set aside for writing. Make it the priority, and don't let anything else pull you away. If you think you don't have enough time, see the next tip.

Try Microwriting

My friend Barbara turned me on to an idea called "micromovements," a concept that suggests that when you take things in small bites and give yourself credit for these little movements, rather than berating yourself for how you didn't do "everything," these small things add up and you're nicer to yourself in the process. So if all you can get done is a page, a sentence, a scene, that's more than you had before. And when you take the pressure off yourself to do a specific set or amount, the muse has a funny way of taking hold of that single sentence or paragraph and running away with it.

Set a Word Count Goal

However, if you are, in fact, motivated by deadlines, then word count goals are elegant, simple, and time-tested. Set a minimal word count, and be amazed at how you're not only more likely to hit it but to exceed it. This is what has made National Novel Writing Month (NaNoWriMo) so wildly popular. All writers must do in order to complete a 50,000-word novel draft in thirty days is use a daily word count goal to urge them on. Most writers I know who have successfully completed NaNoWriMo (myself included) found themselves writing more than the minimum (1,600 words or so) each day. But even a much more minimal word count can help trick you into productivity without pressure. There's no need to be perfect—only prepared to write.

Find an Accountabilibuddy

If you've set up a Creative Support Team, then you probably already have an accountabilibuddy, whether you know it or not (and if not, it's fun to say aloud, no?). When you're feeling the grip of inertia, you might need a writing friend to hold you accountable. Just like in your word count effort, you hold each other to some sort of standard, and cheer and reward each other for getting it done. My accountabilibuddy sends me texts while I'm working and checks in with me about my goals. There's nothing like receiving a little cheerful pressure.

Get to the Heart

Sometimes inertia strikes because you don't want to explore or feel something that the work exposes. When it comes to writing, inertia is often a sign that you must go more deeply into the work, think in a wider direction, or cut something that isn't working. This is especially true if you're writing something personal (though most writing has a personal element, even fiction) and is one of the hardest aspects of writer's inertia to curb. This is when it's good to call on your Creative Support Team or just someone you can talk to. And if talking to others doesn't work for you, then I recommend taking a step away and writing in a journal about the feelings that have created the claws of inertia. If nothing else, it's important to acknowledge that your inertia stems from a personal place so you can be aware of it.

Create Cliff-Hangers

One of the most effective techniques for finding your way back into material you've started is to leave off a writing session midsentence, paragraph, or scene. Creating these cliff-hangers has a way of jogging the brain into finishing that line of dialogue left unresolved or answered, or that scene about to culminate in a high point. It also takes away the burden of having to "finish" everything you write in one sitting.

Finish the Unfinished

Speaking of finishing, think for a second of your own unfinished projects: that roughly drafted NaNoWriMo novel, the short story you intended to send to that contest, the stack of essays you think might make a memoir. They may only physically live on your desk or your laptop, but you may not realize that they also live inside you, in all their impartial nature. They take up psychic residence in your mind, your heart; they're like the cluttered attic of your creative muse. And when the muse is weighed down with what hasn't been completed, it's harder for her to help you create new material.

But what if it's crap? the cranky voice in your head may ask.

Crap (i.e., raw, unpolished words, or words that detour from where you imagined they would go) never turns into creative gold until you finish it. It can't. And you won't ever find out if you're hung up on perfection. Sometimes starting a new project is a form of avoidance. From personal experience, I know that when I have to go deeper, tear something apart, or stretch into new territory, my urge to start a new project hits an all-time high. Finishing is doing the work.

More important, completion brings pride. I always feel a thrill of elation when I finish a draft, even when I know I'm still at an early stage of a project and that I have so much more distance to cover. Because without this draft I have nothing to revise, just a jumble of words in my brain.

Finishing also lets you see the merit and potential of an idea. Yes, some ideas will never reach an audience. But they almost always give birth to other ideas, new avenues. And you test and stretch your skills with every word you write, so something you did as an "experiment" will still pay off in your next project.

Finishing a project is a way of valuing yourself, your work, your words. It allows you to take *you* seriously. It lets you be true to your work. It's also one of the most important steps in building a long-lasting, sustainable writing practice that will give back to you during difficult times.

Finishing frees up head space and creative and emotional energy. Once you get the weight off your head, productivity has a funny way of returning. When you leave a project undone, it stays inside you, a squatter taking up unwanted residence. Finishing comes with an endorphin rush all its own. It's something you can check off that list and give yourself credit for.

Move It

You'll notice that most chapters in this book include a "Move It" section at the end. I'm including this one earlier, because physical movement is effective at shifting energy about 75 percent of the time without employing any other strategies. Thoughts and feelings have a way of getting pressed down too tightly into the cellar of the subconscious, trapped beneath the skin, and have the power to launch you into frustration, anxiety, and discouragement.

"Sweat is like WD-40 for your mind—it lubricates the rusty hinges of your brain and makes your thinking more fluid," says Christopher Bergland, author of *The Athlete's Way: Sweat and the Biology of Bliss*.

Here's the great news: You don't have to be an athlete to take advantage of "exercise" to stimulate your creativity. If you're blocked while sitting at the computer, you need to break your focus. Get up, pace the room, do jumping jacks, or even just walk to another part of the house and take deep breaths. Or, if you're blocked but you have the creative urge, go for a walk or run. Many professional writers break up their workday by adding physical exercise. The list of famous authors who run is quite surprising and includes Joyce Carol Oates, Haruki Murakami, and Laurie Halse Anderson. Having a dog to walk, animals to feed, and children to tend to can often provide crucial break time. When you move your body, you engage the conscious part of your brain in the activity, which wedges open the door to the unconscious, where your creative magic hides.

Meditate

Meditation may seem like nothing more than sitting with your eyes closed while you battle to keep your thoughts from having a wrestling match in your head. But science has taken an interest in discovering what makes Buddhist monks in remote parts of Tibet calmer, less anxious, and more focused, to the point where they are able to withstand intense cold, heat, and other painful sensations. What is it about sitting still that has such a profound effect on our psyches?

Respected institutions from the Mayo Clinic to Harvard University have undertaken studies that reveal that even just a little bit of meditation, from five to fifteen minutes a day, can put your brain into the state most associated with clear, calm, and creative thinking. Not to mention that when you're feeling stuck creatively, sitting quietly without any intention or pressure allows access to the subconscious mind, where creative ideas are often stored.

Daydream or Let Your Mind Wander

If meditation won't work for you in this moment—if you don't feel "ready" to calm down—try this time-tested, imagination-boosting method, practiced by kids all over the globe: daydreaming. It requires no tools, you can do it in any setting, and no one has to know what you're thinking. We spend so much time with our noses buried in computers that send constant streams of data into our minds; in just the decade or so since the birth of the smartphone, we rarely take a break from incoming information. Daydreaming is a form of letting your inner wisdom emerge without pressure. But don't take my word for it. Researcher and psychologist Scott Barry Kaufman co-authored a paper with Rebecca L. Miller called "Ode to Positive, Constructive Daydreaming" for *Scientific American.*

"Daydreaming is a way to 'dip into [your] inner stream of consciousness,' and personally reflect on the world and visualize the future,"

Kaufman says. "This sort of impromptu introspection can even help us to find the answers to life's big questions."

Try daydreaming about your characters and their stories, or about a theme or idea that's haunted you or compelled you to write. Don't give yourself any parameters or rules about what to write, but keep your notebook nearby just in case.

WORK IT

For this chapter on breaking the blocks to creative flow, I'm giving you three different tasks, because your reason for block may not be the same each time, and also because sometimes it takes more than one method to slip inertia's grip.

1. **MENTAL:** Quickly take a look at the work you're stuck on, or simply hold in mind the project you can't start. Or if you have research materials or other info about the project, put it in front of you. Give yourself the goal of writing *one sentence.* That's it, just *one* sentence. Now get up and do the physical activity in exercise two. Then come back. See if you can't write just *one more* sentence. Then get up and do a physical activity. Come back. Write *one more*.

2. **PHYSICAL:** A study done by cognitive psychologist Professor Lorenza Colzato of Leiden University in The Netherlands revealed that people who exercised four times a week were "able to think more creatively than those with a more sedentary lifestyle." But you don't have to run marathons or even leave your house in order to engage in a creativity-stimulating form of exercise. Did you know that simply flapping your arms as though to simulate flying, which also gets your heart rate up, is enough to do the trick? If you can make yourself laugh in the process, even better.

   Make sure no one's around, so you won't do this halfheartedly. Pretend you're a bird. Try to take flight. Even squawk. Maybe you're a chicken. By now, you're either laughing or flapping, and your heart rate is up. Your subconscious creative trapdoor just swung open without you even realizing it. Return to your desk and write *one more sentence.*

3. **EMOTIONAL:** You may have heard about a somewhat dubious-sounding therapeutic technique introduced in the seventies called primal scream therapy. This therapy emerged from the idea that sometimes all a person needs to do to shed emotional baggage is to have a good primal yawp at the top of his lungs. This could also include pillow punching, phonebook ripping, and other feats of brute strength. Don't worry—I'm not going to ask you to do this! I am, however, going to ask you to do a written version of it. Set a timer for fifteen minutes minimum, with no maximum. Whatever works for you. At the top of the page, write what you're facing, whether it's inertia or creative block, in as derogatory language as you can muster: "I can't make progress on my stupid novel."

Below that, start a list called "Reasons I won't/shouldn't/can't make progress with this project." In psychoanalysis, this is called the "pro-symptom" approach. Rather than trying to talk yourself into something you don't want to do, you sympathize with and embrace the discomfort, the part of you throwing its personal tantrum. See how long you can actually go on with this negative sympathy.

When you run out of things to write, start a new list: "Reasons why I should/must/will finish this project." Always try to end an exercise on a positive note.

chapter 11

BE BOLD, WRITE BRAVELY

> *"We have to dare to be ourselves, however frightening or strange that self may prove to be."*
> —MAY SARTON

BUILD YOUR OWN BRAND OF BOLD

You read a lot about "author platform" and "branding" these days. This chapter is about shaping the root of those things—developing your distinguishing, singular imprint on the world as manifested in your writing. In other words, what makes you bold, memorable, fresh?

I'll bet if you were asked to think of "bold" writers, several names would come to mind. They may be boundary-pushing visionaries who say whatever they think. Or they may just be people who write a straightforward, honest truth. They may write things that "average" people don't or that you never thought one could write about. Why you consider them to be bold is indicative of your comfort level with expression. For some people the word *bold* is negative, but I'm using it here to convey a kind of bravery and honesty in your writing. Off the top of my head, I can think of some bold writers from a variety of genres: Toni Morrison, Lena Dunham, Chuck Palahniuk ... writers whose voices are unforgettably unique, brave, and definitely bold.

MAKE NO APOLOGIES

One of the most intriguing hallmarks of bold writers is that they don't apologize for themselves. And nor should you. Don't apologize for the space you take up, your opinions, your perspective, where you come from, or any of your experiences. Writing is a bold act—a declaration of having something to say. While even the boldest writers tremble from time to time after sending something out into the world (in fact, I'd venture, most writers do), they do it anyway and stand behind their work. Being bold is about giving yourself permission to tell and share your stories. And yes, people will criticize, judge, and occasionally get angry at what you've written. Your job is to stand in your truth with courage. The haters and naysayers can write their own stories.

Now, not apologizing for yourself does *not* give you permission to behave cruelly, to wield your boldness like a weapon against others. It doesn't mean you should use your work to write badly about others just because you can. If anything, the boldest, most exposing writing is that which is also compassionate. Bold writing is vulnerable writing.

DARE TO BE VULNERABLE

Boldness may seem to be about toughness on the exterior, but it goes hand in hand with vulnerability and transparency. The "tough" writer is one who has all the same fears as the rest of us but writes what she wants anyway. Being bold is being you but with the veil removed, your edges exposed, and your seams showing. Great writing is not perfect; it's real. It bleeds and leaves a trace.

How vulnerable are you willing to be in your writing? Do you include your real feelings, your personal life? Do you write about emotions you know intimately? In your fiction do you tackle subjects close or foreign to you? Do you find yourself staying in a comfort zone of certain themes or messages out of a fear of saying more? When you experience a shivery little feeling of being "too bold," or bolder than usual, it often results in a pretty spectacular experience for both you and your audience. Readers feel that authentic, vulnerable energy; they know you're giving them something deep and honest. Being bold cements trust with your readers and gives them permission to be so bold, too.

CLAIM YOUR IDENTITY

Boldness is also about claiming the identity of Writer (the capital W is intentional!) and adding it to the top of the other roles you carry rather than relegating it to the side. For many writers, the moment you said to a friend or an audience, "I am a writer," is usually a memorable one, almost a rite of passage or transition. Instead of just "a person who writes" or "dabbles" in writing, you gain power in standing up and asserting that you are not just a hobbyist but a writer for the long haul. A practitioner, if you will.

The reason I call it a writing *practice* instead of a career is that *career* connotes success only in the instance of money or a particular product. But yours is a writing practice no matter what stage you're at, and you have every right (and I strongly encourage you) to claim your writing as important, powerful work even if you've never published a thing. The only requirement of being a writer with a writing practice is that *you keep writing.*

Boldness is also part of the process in learning to tune out the critical voices of others, those forces in league with inertia that want to pull you down and away from your own greatness.

COMBAT SELF-DEPRECATION

No one likes to receive negative comments from others, but the most negative force on your own self-esteem, and thus your bold writing practice, is your own negativity. Read the following sentence, for example.

Your writing is magnificent. I was really moved by your words. You have such a talent for expressing yourself.

What are the first words you hear in your head when you read those words? Do you hear yourself demur, *Oh, not really,* or *But you should read my friend X's words,* or something equally self-deprecating? Or maybe you feel a surge of pride but follow it up by scolding yourself: *Who do you think you are? Don't boast. Aren't you bold!* Those are just a few of the common voices that can be found running on a critical loop in writers' minds. Whether you were raised to be humble to the point of never speaking of your own talents or you're afraid of coming off as "arrogant," you might have a tendency to squash your capacity or dim your brightness, especially if others find it threatening or competitive, or simply don't know how to properly support you. We'll talk in chapter eighteen, "Alleviate Envy," about how sometimes other people's suppressed longing can become misdirected into envy.

You've made strides toward the authenticity that is already yours; that's the first step. But a writing practice is, in many ways, a bold enterprise. Anytime you put thoughts into words is a bold step. You're making form out of idea, concretizing something ethereal, and thus, in your own way, saying: *I matter. My words matter.*

Being bold also means claiming your voice as your own rather than attempting to mimic others'. It means not censoring yourself (at least in the act of drafting—you can revise as needed later), putting your work and yourself in front of an audience, and speaking of yourself honestly, positively, and with conviction.

It took me many years of receiving compliments to learn that a compliment giver hates nothing more than receiving a self-deprecating reply. In a way, deferring your talent or impact is a form of refusing the compliment and thus denying the opinion of the compliment giver as well as giving yourself a backhanded insult. Self-deprecation is a symptom of not giving yourself credit or taking your writing seriously. Sometimes it's a fear of coming off as having a big ego or seeming boastful.

The reasons may be manifold, but the behavior looks the same to the compliment giver and it has the effect of disconnecting the reader, listener, or viewer from the message you're seeking to communicate rather than connecting.

Writing is connecting; even rants, manifestos, and diatribes are attempts to connect. We write and speak to reach and move others, to seek approval, to feel less alone, to incite a discussion, to learn new information, to strike up wonder and awe, and many other reasons. And each stage of connection requires a new level of boldness. It takes one kind of boldness to write in the first place and another kind to share your work, seek feedback, or submit to journals, agents, and publishers.

One of the greatest challenges of my own adventures in education came in my final semester of earning my masters in creative writing. To graduate, I had to give a lecture to the entire student body, faculty, and visiting writers—several hundred people, including some of my literary idols. I spent a lot of time watching other near-graduates, as well as seasoned authors, give their lectures along the way, and I took notes. This is what I came to: When the lecturer communicated his subject as though it was truth—that is, he made eye contact, spoke with authority, moved right past any stumbles or flubs, and stood straight— the lecture, no matter the subject, had an impact on me, stuck in my memory, and left me feeling I'd learned something. In other words, it was the assertiveness, boldness, and confidence of the lecturer that sold me the lecture. I think a similar kind of assertiveness is communicated via your words to readers when you dare to be bold.

THE ART OF PITCHING YOURSELF (EVEN WHEN YOU HAVE TO FAKE IT)

I can't say enough about the "fake it until you make it" approach to building your boldness. Sometimes you have to pretend you feel highly about yourself and your work before you actually feel that way.

Here's the hard truth: Agents, publishers, and readers don't want to know that you don't think you're talented, experienced, polished, or capable enough. They want to believe in you. They want to fall into the "dream" you're selling in words. They want to be seduced.

So much of marketing is about framing and staging information and imagery in a way that appeals to audiences. You will be required to exercise boldness at many stages in your writing practice, even when you're not feeling so bold. Here are a few tips for faking your own boldness until it comes naturally.

Step Up

Part of boldness is mustering courage. And before you say that you're not courageous, remember what courage *is*: It's the ability to rally strength, confidence, certainty, and faith when you don't necessarily feel it. In other words, it's making strength out of a sense of weakness. Or, as I say to my six-year-old son, "Courage is when you're scared but you do the thing you're afraid of anyway." It's choosing to be bold when it would be easier not to. And the avenue to finding that courage is in exposing yourself and looking within. As Brenè Brown says, "Vulnerability is the most accurate measurement of courage."

Aim High

Even if you're not feeling it right now, you probably know what kind of writing you can produce when you're at your best, and you have at least a sense of what your writing reads like when you've penned something stellar. So if you need to pitch yourself or describe yourself or your work, describe *the best version* of you or the work and yourself. Then you're also more likely to hold yourself to that standard.

Trade Out

Still struggling to access your boldness? Trade pitches with a writing friend. Ask someone who knows and likes you and your writing to write about you or your project in glowing terms. See how someone else would describe you or your work. Borrow from that.

WORK IT

Okay, it's time to determine your level of boldness with a set of questions. When you determine what your comfort levels are, you know what "boldness" means to you. Boldness is taking steps outside of your comfort zone. You don't have to take huge, risky steps; you can start with small ones (and we'll talk more about those in chapter thirteen, "Stretch Your Skills,"), but first we start with identifying your current comfort zone.

Answer the following questions with a yes or no. Are you comfortable ...

- revealing personal feelings in your writing?
- showing your failings or humanity?
- publicly sharing your mistakes?
- using strong language?
- writing about taboo subjects?
- writing about people you know?
- showing people your work?
- reading in front of others?
- telling people you are a writer?
- answering the question, "What have you published?"
- answering the question, "Do you get paid for it?"

The number of times you answered yes or no will give you a snapshot of your comfort with "boldness." It's not a road map yet—that is coming in chapter thirteen. But it's a first step, a personal inventory that you'll work with.

MOVE IT

A couple of years back, I participated in my first flash mob, where a bunch of people spontaneously danced to a song in the middle of a downtown Fourth of July festival. When our song came on, thirty of us parted the dense crowd and danced to a number we'd practiced. It was terrifying. And euphoric. People joined in. Strangers clapped. We wound up featured in the local newspaper. Fear transformed into confidence, and I realized that the worst thing that happens when you put yourself out there is that you might feel a little embarrassed, but you also might have some fun.

In lieu of something as dramatic as flash mobbing, consider taking an exercise or dance class that you'd normally never try. My massage therapist recently told me she has taken up drumming—she's learning the Japanese art of taiko, which is a physical and social form of drumming, something she'd always mistakenly believed to be a masculine form because it's related to martial arts. Now she has a new attitude. She says the practice is so energizing she can use drumming in place of coffee or chocolate when she needs an energy boost!

Or maybe you've always wanted to surf or ski or swim, but you lacked the confidence necessary to sign up for that first lesson. When you limit your movements, you limit awareness of yourself, which is crucial to understanding yourself as a writer, too. How you move and hold and carry yourself has a lot to do with your experiences. The more you know about you, the more you can translate that onto the page.

chapter 12

INCREASE YOUR CRAFT

"It is failure that guides evolution; perfection provides no incentive for improvement, and nothing is perfect."
—COLSON WHITEHEAD, FROM *THE INTUITIONIST: A NOVEL*

All writers experience the frustration of being unable to steer a piece of writing in the direction they want it to go. You don't get the story "right," so you crumple up the pages and toss them across the room (or smack your laptop or yell at your iPad). Or maybe you've worked on a short story for months or even years, and you still can't bear to submit it. After all, it might not be "done" yet. You've spent all this time shaping and reshaping that one piece, and it still isn't finished and thus your critical voices say you must have failed.

You haven't failed. Let me reassure you: Your work will never feel done, not even after it's bound between two book covers on a bookstore shelf. Writers don't ever finish work; they just let it go. You are not a failure because your large, bold vision didn't easily distill into a finished work with just one pass. But for those of you who can't even get to the "letting go" stage because of one of the following reasons, this chapter is for you.

- I don't have a college degree in creative writing.
- I can't afford and/or make time for writing classes.

- I don't know who to trust with critiquing my work.
- If I start revising, I'll never stop.
- I can't afford an editor.
- I can't trust anyone to give me honest feedback.
- All the writing guides give contradictory advice.
- I'm going to self-publish, so I don't need to do as much work.

Do any of these reasons sound familiar? No matter where you are in your level of writing craft, there is always another lesson to learn, and that should be a welcome feeling; it means you can continually learn to improve and polish your work and impress yourself (not to mention readers) with your level of craft.

It's okay to be ambivalent about feedback, and lack of money and time are very real issues. But writing is a craft, which means you need not be perfect right this moment; you can continue to hone it. And the more you work on your craft—that is, the time you spend consciously apprenticing yourself to become better at your area of writing—the more invested you will feel in your writing practice and the more it will shine with the burnish of your hard work.

BUSTING COMMON WRITING MYTHS

In the rest of this chapter, we'll tackle the common myths writers use to put off pursuing the craft and break each myth open to show you it's possible to improve, no matter what your obstacles.

Myth: Some Writers Just Have "Natural Talent"

Time and time again I've seen a popular artistic myth stymie writers: You either have "it"—meaning natural writing talent—or you don't. Those with "it" go on to be successful and famous, the myth states, while the rest flounder in obscurity. That is utterly false. The most successful writers are not always the most "inherently talented" but rather the most persistent, who work the hardest at their craft. Lots of talented writers let their demons squash their art and do not persist at the practice, devote time to the craft, or pursue publication. I've worked with students and clients over the years who started out writing middle school–equivalent pieces only to improve their craft with dedication and persistence to publishable quality. And I've also worked with those who let a few hard words halt them in their tracks.

Frankly, believing that you must be "talented" before you even start is a form of procrastination. If you believe you can't or won't improve, there's no motivation to get started or keep at it. Don't give up so easily. Remember that you are called to write for one reason or another. Maybe you have only one story in you, or hundreds. Quantity is not important, but commitment to your craft is, not just for the product you may produce but for your personal fulfillment.

Myth: No Money, No Time

We all live in the real world of material objects and responsibilities. Most of you do not have a large sum of disposable income lying around, and you may not want to take on debt to attend a writing program. What's a writer to do?

There's this marvelous invention—you may have heard of it—called The Internet. And on this Internet are some truly wondrous *free* opportunities for writers to improve their craft.

Before I ever thought that earning a graduate degree in writing was a remote possibility for both time and money concerns, I scouted out local writing groups via my college bulletin, my local paper, and arts and entertainment magazines. In the years before I earned an MFA, I took "classes" led by hardworking writers who didn't teach at universities but wanted a writing community: in a barn, in a granny unit, in a warehouse, in more than a few coffee shops, in several living rooms, on a beach, in a yurt, in a jazz lounge, and even in someone's car. I hungered for knowledge and improvement, and when local options weren't enough, I joined a listserv group for writers. I think I found it through an Internet search or on a flier at my college. At that time there were no avatars or photos, no video chat, no fancy profiles full of photos and information. We were all just represented by names, in text, on a white screen, like so:

JordanR: Hey, what are your thoughts on first-person point of view?

SamanthaA: I love it. I use it all the time. See?

For an entire year I conducted writing-related conversations with faceless friends, exchanged feedback, and learned a whole heck of a lot without spending more than a few bucks for coffee or gas.

As you well know, since 1999 the online world has exploded with life and depth that none of us could have fathomed at the time. And now, with just a few keystrokes, you can find a bevy of writing resources for low to no cost. Here are just a few.

- **ONLINE WRITING GROUPS:** www.Zoetrope.com, Backspace.com, WriterUnboxed.com. Also, Facebook is swimming with groups for writers of all stripes, genres, and interests. Simple searches will reveal literally thousands you can request to join.
- **ONLINE PEER REVIEW SITES:** www.CritiqueCircle.com, Scribophile.com
- **CRITIQUE SERVICES, DEVELOPMENTAL EDITORS, INDIE PUBLISHING ADVICE, AND WRITING COACHES:** Writer's Digest's "Second Draft" editing and critique services (www.writersdigestshop.com/author-service-center/writing-critique-service), Scribendi.com, TheBookDesigner.com
- **BLOGS BY WRITERS FOR WRITERS:** ElizabethSpannCraig.com, HelpingWritersBecomeAuthors.com, www.LiveWriteThrive.com, TerribleMinds.com

When browsing online, you can also refine your search to the most specific criteria.

"writers' group for paranormal writers of romance (vampire)"

"editors of historical sweet westerns"

Or, better yet, if you know the area of craft you need to work on but don't especially care to work with others, try a search on a specific area of craft.

"tips on point of view for fiction writers"

"writing strong scenes for memoir"

There are so many quick and easy resources for online classes now. Some writers even offer free webinars and mini-courses via their blogs. There are so many, in fact, that I'm not going to make you a list, but I do recommend that you search for a particular area of craft, check for testimonials, and ask other writers where they've taken classes. Online classes often have live components in the form of video, audio, or chat streaming (or all three) and can simulate a "live" classroom with a great deal of accuracy. Even classes with static chat boards offer self-paced interaction that holds you accountable to deadlines and offers instructor critique.

All in all, you have more free and inexpensive methods of improving your craft at your disposal than you can spend the rest of your life taking advantage of. There's no excuse not to improve, both for the sake of producing a result that makes your work better and for the interpersonal satisfaction, discovery, and joy that comes as a result of working hard.

The information is out there. No excuses.

Myth: Improving Your Craft Is Grueling

It's true: Work, and specifically improvement of your writing craft, is hard in contrast to not trying to improve at all. But that doesn't mean that improving your craft is grueling, miserable work. It can even be fun.

Not improving doesn't take any effort, though it does take a mental and emotional toll to sit on unfinished, unresolved writing that you wrote in a burst of inspiration, passion, or purpose. When you leave things left undone, it puts the taste of regret and longing on your palette. I know a few people who left their writing dreams by the wayside to pursue other careers, and their regret lingers like a faint trace of smoke around them always. You write your life as you would any other story—it's your choice. No one will force you to write.

But if you keep the following things in mind, it will make the work of writing and improving less strenuous—and far more enjoyable.

- You don't have to be perfect.
- You only have to do a little at a time.
- You only have to show your work to your trusted Creative Support Team.
- You don't even have to leave your house.
- You can work in your pajamas.
- You can write a few words a day between work and family obligations.
- You're not obligated to make a career; you're simply adding another mile to your writing practice.
- Creative arts are good for the spirit, the emotions, and the body.

Myth: Self-Published Authors Don't Need to Work as Hard on Craft

Writers who plan to self-publish often feel that they need less craft technique, but this is not only untrue, it's also a bit of an insult to your own best effort. I have a lot more to say about self-publishing in chapter twenty-three, "Go It Alone," but for now, consider this: In the life of a book produced by a mainstream publisher, a team of people in addition to the writer is responsible for its birth, production, and quality. Editors, copy editors, designers, and publicists all stand as partial parents in the life of the book.

Self-publishing reflects primarily on one person: you. If a mainstream book suffers typos or some problem with content, people might say, "I can't believe that author's editor let her leave that in."

Someone other than the writer may have influenced the final result. In self-publishing there's no one but you at the front line—sure, you may also have a team behind you, but the public won't know that. Which means that the work you send into the world (and I have become a strong advocate for independent publishing in the right ways and at the right time) is, in essence, your vision of your best work at the time. That doesn't mean you don't have room to learn or grow, but it does mean that if you decide to self-publish in lieu of improvement, your audience will pick up on that. And it will only reflect poorly on you.

As I said above, there are no excuses not to find the information you need or the readers, critique partners, and editors that will help you take your work to the next level; it's all out there at your fingertips. You would be amazed at what an online search will reveal.

You might be asking: Why should I bother to polish and improve my craft at all? What's wrong with the raw, unkempt ideas that come to me on muse-born drafts of inspiration? My answer to that is: Nothing at all. But if you seek to connect your work to an audience, then you are, in essence, making your readers a promise that you will guide them toward a particular kind of experience in a satisfying way. Perhaps the experience you're offering has a predetermined label: Romance Novel or Short Story or Historical Fiction. Whichever it is, once you lead readers to the marquee, you are now in charge of making good on that feature. Writing, in other words, has rules. Rules that can be bent and manipulated by deft hands, and rules that are, I must say, extraordinarily fun to both learn and break. But they are rules that need to be learned and applied nonetheless. And how do you get to engage in this kind of literary play? By improving your craft.

Myth: There's Too Much Writing Advice

Where do I start learning all this valuable craft when I'm so overwhelmed?

You start by choosing a technique you are either interested in working on or that you know you are capable of working on at that time and place. You don't have to learn everything at once. But like a toddler, your muse will probably be most committed if you start with an issue that interests you rather than one you feel you "must" learn. Whether the topic is plot structure or strong dialogue, if you're committed to the path, it almost doesn't matter where you start.

Then look to books, classes, online writing groups, other writers, and so on. Ask questions. By doing so, you invoke a spirit of willingness to learn by doing. You don't have to be an expert already.

I also suggest you read widely and often, and emulate the writers you love. Analyze books: What do they do that is so compelling? How do the authors craft their stories?

Put down the writing advice guides that don't speak to you and hold tight to the ones that do. You don't need to follow *all* the wisdom you encounter, only that which actually makes you feel wiser.

WHEN TO HIRE A PAID EDITOR OR BOOK COACH

How do I know when it's time to pay someone to edit my work?

The answer to that question, which I give at conferences and workshops is: You hire an editor or book coach when you are ready to spend money to hear that you have more work to do. That may sound obvious, but I've met many a writer who hired an editor as a last step to validation, as if the stamp of approval would mean she could now safely publish. If you are *not* totally clear that hiring an editor means you will have more work to do, then you are not ready.

You might also hire someone when you're stuck. For instance, you might receive contradictory feedback from your critique group that says vastly differing things or consistent feedback that highlights a problem you don't know how to fix. A freelance editor or coach can provide you with an unbiased, learned perspective.

I've worked as an editor, a writing coach, and a writing teacher for over a decade, and I regularly exhort new writers and students to interview me until they feel satisfied that I am the right person for their job. You have the right to ask all the questions you need answered before you hand over money or sign a contract to have someone apply their personal opinion to your precious work.

This is an intimate relationship; you're entrusting your work, and possibly paying money, to someone who will point out the flaws. The very structure of this relationship is fraught with potential issues. It's as tender a relationship as the one you have with a therapist or a doctor, and as such, one you should enter with care.

What you want, at the end of the day, is someone you trust enough that you feel motivated to take his or her advice.

Interview Tips for Hiring an Editor

First, keep in mind the primary truth of hiring an editor: You're spending money to have someone tell you that you have more work to do. You may think me silly for putting that in writing—twice, no less—but let me tell you, every editor I've interviewed has had clients who believed that the editor's role was to pat the writer on the back for how well he's done. I know writers who were offended at the idea that they had more work to do and were insulted that they'd paid money to learn this fact. That is why I recommend hiring an editor at a late stage in the process.

Ask a lot of questions of your prospective editor, starting with these.

- How much do you charge?
- What is your projected turnaround time for my project?
- Do you offer a sample edit for a discount?
- How will you make your edits? Digitally, in track changes, or on hard copy?
- In what form can I expect comments?
- Do you use a contract? (Always go for a contract so you know exactly what you're getting for your money, as well as reimbursement policies.)

It's also smart to get referrals from the editor's clients. And remember that it's only one person—no matter how skilled. If the editor's opinion doesn't feel right, trust your gut.

WORK IT

1. Identify an area of writing craft for which you know, or have been told, you could use some improvement. Choose from one of the suggestions in this chapter: Join a critique group—more on that in chapter sixteen, "Combat Criticism, Seek Critique"— or find a free online course, webinar, or writing group to participate in. Participate with the intention of improving only one area of your craft. When you begin to notice improvement, pick a new area to get support for.

2. Here's a fun exercise: Take a book you've loved that has a strong voice or style *different* from your own. Now write a paragraph of your own story in that same voice or style. If I were to do this, I'd use Cormac McCarthy's *No Country for Old Men*, since I tend to write long, flowing sentences, heavy on the imagery, whereas he is terse, spare, and succinct. Yet his books are evocative and dramatic in a way I would love my own to be. Try to identify what it is about the author that is so unique. Does he write in short staccato sentences? Is the character a smack-talking bad boy? Does the writer use lots of metaphor and imagery? When you play with the style of another writer and adapt your own work to it (just as an exercise), you teach yourself a new skill in a subconscious way, without the rational mind telling you you're doing it wrong.

MOVE IT

Take a walk to the nearest local library, bookstore, or newsstand. The goal here is to get you up and out, but with a destination in mind. Buy or check out a book or magazine on writing craft, or even a literary journal that appeals to you, particularly if it offers information in an area you have been wanting to explore. While you're there, select a book that's different from what you usually read, one you think you can learn from.

chapter 13

STRETCH YOUR SKILLS

"If you dare nothing, then when the day is over, nothing is all you will have gained."

—NEIL GAIMAN, FROM *THE GRAVEYARD BOOK*

Writers walk a fine line between comfort and risk. On the side of comfort are the rules, the formulas, and the known path that helps you chart a course, find an audience, and refine your voice. On the side of risk is everything else. That's where you walk precariously on a bridge over rough waters, crack open calcified parts of your psyche, tap into universal themes from surprising angles, and do what artists do best (and yes, I consider writers artists): reveal, discover, expose, voice, connect.

But every writer has her comfort zone. You know which territory you're happiest traveling in, and perhaps you've never ventured beyond it. That doesn't mean it's the only place you should explore. This chapter is about stretching yourself creatively as well as courageously. A successful writing practice is a brave enterprise, made braver in the face of a culture that often demands you show proof in the form of money or goods. It may take years before you have either wealth or tangible reward to show for your practice, but every day you should do something to expand the boundaries of your practice, widen your circle, and open your net. Every day you have something to show yourself and your muse, and that will count for so much more than you can ever quantify in dollars or units.

Since you may not be the kind of writer who actively pursues risks, the best way to find them is to stay aware of "adventure opportunities" and say yes to them every time. How do you know you are taking a risk? You may feel terror, uncertainty, bewilderment, euphoria, anxiety, or fear of being found out as a fraud.

But don't run away at the first sign of these feelings. Risks don't feel "easy." Easy is rarely a part of the artist's experience, I'm afraid. Ease is for later, after you've taken risks and stretched. Ease is the cool-down period.

Saying yes means staying open. Opportunities might at first seem more like challenges, and thus you may simply pass them by or say no. But saying yes has many, many benefits. For one thing, especially in the case of volunteer efforts, you're often given access to skills and connections you might not otherwise get. When I was called on to start a volunteer literary radio show for a small local station, I had never been on the air, much less inside a radio station, in my life. I was nervous about whether I could pull off such a thing. But I was drawn to the idea of engaging with writers on my favorite topics. So I took the leap, palms sweating all the way, voices crying "fraud" inside my head.

And there were plenty of shaky moments. My producer created a reel of "outtakes" for my birthday one year, of all the hilarious and frustrating moments when I lost my cool, fumbled a title or an author's name, or pulled a Casey Kasem and swore a blue streak.

I made no money for my efforts, but I did gain access to the very people I most admired: authors. Well-known, occasionally even *New York Times* best-selling authors, some of whom came into the studio and sat in front of me. (Others were conducted via "ISDN" line—high-quality digital communication lines that allow conversations between studios to sound as if they are happening in the same studio.) I'll never forget T.C. Boyle's robust flyaway hair and his red Converse sneakers, or the way I found Aimee Bender on her back in a yoga pose on the floor when I came in, or the time I sat knee to knee in the back office of a bookstore with Louise Erdrich, whose books were among those that made me want to take up the mantle of a writer as a young girl. Holding the position of interviewer forced me to read critically, to think up interesting questions, and to analyze the craft. It was a mini fiction course in and of itself. I spent hours and hours of my time producing an hour-long show that aired twice a month and probably only reached people within a one hundred-mile radius. And yet it was one of the most profound experiences of my life. It stretched me, connected me to kindred spirits, and taught me a lot. When I later had an opportunity to do book commentaries for KQED Radio for pay, I was able to bring these skills to bear. And besides, beneath the work and the labor, it was fun.

Remember in chapter eight when we talked about going where you are welcome? Opportunities that will stretch you come with a buzzing feeling of possibility tinged with a little fear. Most of the time, fear is good. It's a fear that will push you to rise above, to shoot for your personal best. But if fear paralyzes you, that's a different story. In chapter two we talked about your comfort zone and how only you know what you're willing to risk. You don't need to take risks that will set you back—only those that will pry open new corners of yourself.

You may balk at an opportunity, thinking you have to be some kind of expert, only to find out that all you need to be is yourself—present and attentive.

When it's time to say yes to a new opportunity that inspires that thrill of fear, before you say no, remember to turn to your Creative Support Team: Often they can act as a sounding board as you embark on this new step or activity.

I also highly recommend saying yes to opportunities to write in a new way or for a new publication, audience, or blog. Putting your work, or yourself, in front of new eyes always leads to good things. Writers have told me time and time again (and I have experienced it myself as well) that trying out new things, from events to writing opportunities, leads to unexpected bounty in other ways. I'll say more about this in chapter fifteen, "Consider No Effort Wasted," but trust me when I say that all the seeds you plant now, no matter how small, will reap some fruit eventually if you keep at your writing practice.

When you're presented with a new opportunity, consider the following.

- Can you fit it into your life by carving out something less important?
- What new skills or connections will it bring?
- Will it look good on your résumé or credentials?
- Will it lend you literary credibility?
- Will it be fun or exciting?

GET SMART

If you're still not convinced you should try new things, consider the biological motivation for taking risks. Columbia scientist Eric Kandel earned the 2000 Nobel Prize in Physiology and Medicine (with Arvid Carlsson and Paul Greengard) for his discovery that repeated activation, or practice, causes the synapses of the brain to "swell and make stronger connections," according to John Ratey, M.D. in his book *Spark: The Revolutionary New Science of Exercise and the Brain.* In other words, learning something new and then practicing it makes your brain smarter and stronger. And stronger, smarter brains hold up better over time in old age, are more resistant to dementia and Alzheimer's, and generally retain memories better.

For writers, your brain is your biggest and most important muscle. Sure, you might master something—maybe you can turn out killer romance novels or concise articles on any subject—but doing the same thing again and again leads to mental atrophy and, for many creative types, boredom. Don't let yourself become bored with your work. You should go deeper into your writing practice the longer you're at it, which means opening new avenues and exploring new frontiers, be they genres, forms (novel versus memoir), or subjects.

CREATE YOUR OWN RISKS

Some writers don't need to wait for opportunities to say yes; they are instead motivated to go out and create risk for themselves. I love Neil Gaiman's quote at the beginning of this chapter. There's nothing wrong with comfort, and there's no shame in staying safe, but few changes occur within safety. Life is too short to stay the same, don't you think?

Here's my first rule of risk taking: Decide where you want to go, or what your goal is, and choose to go after it no matter what "they" or "the rules" say. This doesn't mean that you should be rude, foolish, or impractical. It means, for instance, that if the general wisdom is something like "Publishers only take agented submissions," don't take anybody's word for it; find out for yourself. Many smaller publishers will actually read unagented submissions, and some big publishers even have small windows of time in which they are specifically open to unagented submissions. Sending an e-mail won't blackball you from the industry. You have less to lose than to gain. Often these rules are in place to discourage the "masses" who refuse to devote the time and effort to their craft from sending in shoddy work. But you won't do shoddy work. If you decide to tackle an avenue because you feel it's right for you, you'll polish your work until it's blindingly bright, you'll do your research, and you'll leap.

Jonathan Maberry, a prolific and well-loved science fiction and horror writer who is famed for his zombie novels, confirmed this sentiment in a keynote speech he gave at the Central Coast Writers' Conference in 2011. If one of his pitches was rejected, he would often send it to the same editor under a new title—and have it accepted. His point? "No" is subjective. Timing is everything. And you never know if you don't keep trying.

EXPERIMENT WITH FORMS AND GENRES

As a writer, your forte may be fiction or you may be a freelance journalist. Maybe you're a memoirist, or perhaps you're just writing whatever comes out of your mind and you aren't so worried about labels. In any case, there's a good chance you focus on one kind of writing more than another. But some comfort zones are good, and some are overly safe. The good comfort zone keeps you from being pushy with agents at conferences and getting sucked in by vanity presses that just want your money. The overly safe comfort zone is a place of boredom, a lackluster realm where your ideas don't feel interesting and your work doesn't excite you. The latter is a dangerous place for a writing practice, which needs to keep an edge of mystery and freshness about it. That's what artists do, after all: They give new voice to the ordinary aspects of life.

You now know that learning new things creates new synapses in the brain, which leads to new ways of thinking and creating—so you have nothing to lose by learning something new. If pride is your issue—say you've become so adept at writing fiction that you're afraid to look like a "newbie" in the realm of personal essay—that's just the ego trying to exert control over your creative mind. Don't let it. Stretching into a new form is exciting and exhilarating. You open doors to chests full of hidden riches you didn't know were there. And the best part is that sometimes what you find in the new form can be applied to your favorite genre or form. For instance, if you have mastered fictional techniques like scene and character development, you have a leg up when working on memoir, because you know how to activate your writing and bring it to life in a way that some memoir writers struggle with.

Or maybe you realize that the truth you discover in a part of your real life can be deftly molded into the weirder world of fiction.

Short story writers learn they have more stamina for writing when they tackle a long-term project such as a novel.

Stuck novelists discover the short story is an excellent way to feel "accomplished" without having to write three hundred pages.

Journalists bring their methodical eye for detail to writing rich, beautiful scenes.

If you haven't yet experimented with form, you don't know what you stand to gain and how this might stretch your writing to entirely new cosmos.

FIND NEW AUDIENCES

Just because you are comfortable or familiar with one way of reaching people doesn't mean you have to stick to that medium. Many writers who have never tried blogging are surprised to realize that people—strangers—are reading their words. If you've only ever been published in newspapers and are on the receiving end of critical complaints or don't get any feedback at all, making contact with your readers can be a truly heady experience.

Maybe it's time to try a Tumblr blog, post snapshots of your work on Pinterest or Instagram, or even just create a Facebook author page. People are out there waiting to hear what you have to say, but you have to seek them out.

MOVE IT

You might notice that this "Move It" exercise appears before the "Work It" exercise in this chapter when it's usually the other way around. That's because doing moderate exercise thirty minutes before you set out to learn something new is shown to improve memory retention and the speed of synapses firing. So before you go on to the "Work It" exercise, get your body moving. "Exercise influences learning directly, at the cellular level, improving the brain's potential to log in and process new information," says John Ratey, M.D., co-author of *Spark*. The good news is that you don't have to do vigorous exercise to benefit. This chapter suggests you engage in some vigorous stretching.

- Do a series of active stretches such as windmills, high knees, or static lunges.
- Or try a simple flow of yoga poses: tree pose to forward fold to downward dog will do. You can also go further into a plank, cobra pose, and then back up into forward fold and tree pose again. If you aren't familiar with these poses, a quick YouTube or Google search will provide plenty of info, including videos.

WORK IT

1. After you've stretched, answer each of these questions.

- What's your preferred form or genre to write in; i.e., the one you feel most comfortable in?
- What's your next favorite?
- What's the form or genre you've always been curious to experiment with but haven't yet?
- Which form or genre seems incredibly different or hard to you?

Can you guess where this is going? Give one of these new, scarier forms a try. I recommend you really stretch and go with the fourth entry on your list, but any will do.

2. Try your hand at a short essay. Write a fictional account of a true event. Turn a bad day into a horror story. Take a warm moment and channel it into a poem. But please pick the one that feels a little bit challenging so you leave your comfort zone.

chapter 14
RELISH
REVISION

"In the most aesthetically expansive sense, revision is
the opportunity we give ourselves in our writing to 'see
it all again,' more fully, richly, deeply."
—DAVID MICHAEL KAPLAN

Many writers resist revision because it feels hard, they don't know where to start, or it touches that nerve in them that says, "If I didn't do it right the first time, I must not be any good at it." Learning to treat your writing as a practice may be a new way of approaching your craft altogether. If you've been conditioned by the Myth of Overnight Success or you're suffering a bout of perfectionism, you may struggle with the belief that revising means that you have failed or didn't do it well enough the first time.

You have not failed. If you don't have revisions to make, you may be some sort of genius or savant, in which case you probably don't need any of my pep talks. Revision is not a sign of weakness; it's merely a product of the truth that very little is built, constructed, or finished in one pass. This is why I chose to quote David Michael Kaplan at the beginning of this chapter. The full quote discusses revision as literally "re-seeing" one's work. When you look again, you almost always see something you missed. In fact, the more times you "look," the more you may see to change. And that's okay. Writing evolves with time, attention, and feedback.

If you've ever painted a room or a house, you know that you must apply multiple coats or else there are tiny little holes (known by painters as "holidays"—how's that for a literary description?) that make the overall paint job look shoddy. Technically a painter could call a room done after the first coat, but once it dries, it would look half-finished. The same goes for writing.

No matter what you write, writing has many layers to attend to: language, scene, character, plot, voice, style, theme, and more. Nobody can be expected to perfect so many things in one fell swoop.

Add to this the pressure many writers feel, for various reasons, to finish projects and rush their work into the marketplace (in part due to the rise of self-publishing), and revision remains the most unloved, yet crucial, part of the writing craft.

As a writing teacher and coach, my experience is that revision is one of the most persistently difficult areas to get writers to learn to love or enjoy. In part I think this is because many people feel overwhelmed and don't know how to break down the revision process into manageable stages. But once you do learn to love it, or at least embrace it, you will be amazed at how it changes your relationship to your own words. Nothing is more gratifying than watching your idea come together, flesh out, and reach its potential. The rest of this chapter will explore important steps to take on your road to loving revision.

In chapter two I talked about an artist who painted "miles of canvas" on her way to creating a final piece. Writers must write "libraries of words" before they complete a truly finished project. Even if you are a beacon of shining, raw talent, you probably have a trick or two to learn, a habit to curb, or a new way of writing that you'd like to try out. The more you polish your work by putting it through revisions, the better: First drafts can be written in a rush, but subsequent drafts need time.

REVISE YOUR VIEW OF WORK

On Pinterest I came across this quote: "I'm a writer, which just means that writing is harder for me than it is for other people." Obviously it's meant as a joke—except that it isn't one, really. You write because you love it and you're good at it, and you also likely struggle, wrestle, and grapple with it more than someone who only writes occasionally. The struggle means that you're working hard and venturing somewhere new rather than staying complacent. (I think we're far too preoccupied with ease. Where did this notion of art being easy come from? Perhaps somewhere between the advent of fast food and online shopping.)

Let me give you an analogy about why work is good. Last year I planted a garden in my yard. Wait, let me rephrase that. Last year I turned a patch of hard, unyielding dirt into two 5' × 9' raised planter beds. My husband helped me with the hard labor of building the boxes, but the rest was on me. When the truck dumped 3 cubic yards of soil in my driveway and I looked at my lone wheelbarrow and shovel, I experienced a shiver of fear: This was going to be *Work*, with a capital W, and there would be sweat and muscle aches and whining involved. For two hours straight I shoveled dirt into the wheelbarrow until my shoulders burned and throbbed. And then, bracing myself with all the core strength I could muster, I wheeled and dumped thirty or forty loads of soil into the beds until my abs screamed for mercy.

And then? Then I had to rake out the dirt so that it wasn't just sitting there in big piles. Oh, and though it was only early spring, we had a freak heat wave. I started in the relative cool of 9:00 A.M., and by noon it was 80°F.

Here's the thing: I sweated, I groaned, I made gym-rat whoops of effort to push through fatigue. I wore dirt like a second skin. But every bit of the act of gardening felt right, like a skill I'd once had and was remembering. When my seedlings were in at the end of the day, I surveyed my garden, which had once been nothing but dirt but was now a vivid patch of growth in progress, and I felt rewarded.

Revising your writing is a lot like gardening for the mind. There is good, hard work involved, but when approached with the right attitude and in the right way for you, that hard work (revision) is bolstering, healing, and transformative. Once you bust through inertia—the "don't wannas" and the "it's too hards"—you will hit your stride, a place where material takes new shape, comes alive, and transforms into something bigger and better than what you started with.

BRING YOUR VISION TO LIFE

There's really nothing quite as white-hot and powerful as the moment your Grand Idea hits you—meteoric, seismic in its power. But you probably get this idea at the edge of sleep, in the middle of a work meeting, or quite suddenly, without the means to jot it down. By the time you begin in earnest to translate your vision from etheric realm to paper, it comes out like some waifish little runt with mange.

Don't despair! All great art must start in humble form. In the act of chasing the Grand Idea, you do in fact begin to catch up to it, even grow your capacity to write it in the process.

Unfortunately life is not like the movie *The Matrix*; you can't plug in and download the knowledge you need in a few minutes. And writing is an act of discovery as much as it is one of creation.

Revision, then, is making good on that divine initial spark of inspiration. Revision is the chase, and you must not stop until the world on the page is as close to that original vision as possible—and the truly magic part is that the story might become something else in the process, something more: an even Grander Idea or an entirely new one.

That said, I know revision is still difficult. So here are several strategies for you to follow.

Get Necessary Distance

In order to see your work with even the slightest bit of objectivity, you need to spend some time away from it. When you write, you enter the realm of your words, you become your characters, you live your ideas, and you become affected by them. After writing the first draft, you are often too close to your work to be able to see it with any amount of clarity. These words are still just beating, bleeding parts of your being. You need to take time away from your draft before you can revise. Every writer has a different need for distance, but I guarantee you won't be able to kill any darlings, sections, or sentences until you've put the work away for a while. For me that time frame can range from a week to a year. You'll need to find your own happy place.

Take Inventory

When you are finally ready to look at your work as clearly as you are able (you'll never see it as clearly as someone else can), I suggest taking a quick inventory, especially if you've written a book-length work. In an inventory, you break down each scene or chapter into its ingredients. I prefer to make a matrix in Microsoft Excel or similar. (Some people like to use Scrivener or Master Writer.) Inventory the contents of every scene and place them in your graph.

SCENE NUMBER OR NAME	3
WHO: CHARACTER POV	Harry Potter
WHAT: PLOT EVENT	Gets letter to Hogwarts
WHERE: PLOT EVENT	At the Dursley's House
WHY: CONSEQUENCE	He doesn't know he's a wizard yet
WHEN: TIME/DAY	Daytime
RESULT OF SCENE	Uncle throws away letters

For a memoir, you would follow approximately the same method, except that your character is you, the narrator, and your "plot event" is a real event that happened (though it's actually helpful to think of your story in terms of plot). For a nonfiction book other than a memoir, you would state the essential ideas outlined in each chapter. This becomes a working outline you can use to help you revise.

Once you have made a complete graph of your scenes, you have a working outline that boils your manuscript down to a grid. You'll instantly notice if your story has plot holes, if your protagonist isn't showing up in enough scenes, if you've skipped over a chunk of time, and whether each scene leads to a compelling consequence or result. You can also use this grid to move scenes around and rewrite.

Seek Feedback

In my years as a radio host and columnist for *Writer's Digest* magazine, every published author I interviewed revealed they had a writing partner, a writing critique group, or an editor they worked closely with. They did not rely solely on their own eyes to catch what wasn't working. Because they sought feedback, these authors also revised their work based on others' input. Some of them did many, many revisions. I firmly believe that real writing—real craft and certainly polish—happens in the revision. And often revision is more fruitful and effective if it is based, at least in part, on the feedback of others.

Edit in Waves

Don't let the idea of multiple drafts terrify you. You don't rebuild the house from scratch with each revision; you build upon the changes you made in the last round. I recommend you pick a series of craft elements to focus on in each pass. Here are some key areas to revise as you go through. (Remember that memoir draws heavily upon fictional elements of the craft, so the information that follows applies to memoir writers as well. Instead of "character," however, you call yourself the "narrator." Instead of a "plot" you have a "narrative arc." You still write in scenes, using action and dialogue when possible, and at the sentence level, fiction and memoir must adhere to similar rules of style and grammar.)

1. **STRUCTURE**: Determine the backbone of your plot or narrative arc first, so that the high and low points are in the right places. Don't worry about prettying it up yet.

2. **SCENES**: Make sure you have fully fleshed-out scenes—action, dialogue, setting and sensory descriptions, character/narrator interactions, and plot information—and not just pages of exposition and backstory.

3. **CHARACTER**: Make sure your dialogue and character/narrator actions are realistic and appropriate, and that they deepen the reader's understanding of him or her.

4. **IMAGERY AND TENSION**: Be sure to use powerful imagery that creates emotion and tension on every page.

5. **SENTENCES**: Clip out annoying adverbs and adjectives and unnecessary dialogue tags. Replace "he felt" with imagery and sensory description; cut uses of the verb "to be." Check for passive voice, too many gerunds (verbs ending in -*ing*), and run-on sentences. Look for repetition and extra words, such as *it was, there were, began to, started to,* and *continued.*

6. **READ IT ALOUD**: Before you call a book done, always read the whole work aloud; you'll catch inconsistencies you could never catch with the eye alone.

Take Pleasure in the Polish

You know that satisfying smoothness of a piece of weathered beach glass, or the way a polished stone glides beneath your fingers? As water shapes and polishes glass or stone, revision does the same to your words. Surely you turned to writing because some part of you loves to turn words over in the tumbler of your mind, to clip and tease the cadence of your sentences until they gleam. There's nothing so grand to a writer as the feeling of a perfect sentence slipping into place. Have you lost touch with this sensation? Go read some poetry, listen to well-crafted song lyrics, or just watch some episodes of a masterfully plotted show with razor-sharp writing, like *True Detective*.

Language is an elastic and powerful force that moves and bends as you play with it. Don't stay stuck in monotonous, one-note uses of whatever language you're writing in. Push and pull; play and break your words. Learn to hear the way sentences move, and then arrange and rearrange them—scenes, dialogue, and descriptions—until your writing feels as layered and textured as a tapestry.

Don't Rush

For writers, publication feels like a constantly receding horizon you're always chasing. It's easy to give in to the fear that if you don't submit or self-publish *right now* you'll lose an opportunity. But guess what makes a successful author? Care and attention to the writing. The stronger your work, the greater your chances of success. Rushing only leads to sloppiness, which is a major tell to agents, publishers, and even readers that you're unprepared. Your fate, your perfect timing, aren't going anywhere; your writing will find its place when the work is right, and you'll feel a heck of a lot better about it then.

Self-publishing is a wonderful method that I am strongly in favor of when the time is right. But its rise in popularity has also contributed to a false sense of urgency in writers to get work out and done, especially if they're publishing serial fiction. I don't care if you write a book per month; nothing is ever done after a first draft. Nothing.

Your first draft is for telling yourself the story; further drafts shape your work for readers. Don't become complacent with "good enough," especially when people are paying for your work. Rise above. Shine.

WORK IT

Choose a scene or a chapter or a paragraph that is in the first-draft stage (or write a fresh one). You're going to do three drafts (it's okay if you break this up over several days). Follow these steps.

1. Make sure all the elements of a scene are included: The character has an obvious, consistent point of view; your sensory descriptions and imagery show setting and emotion; the action creates a sense of real-time movement and/or dialogue, and a plot goal is present, some piece of which is apparent in this scene.
2. Cut all flabby, extraneous language, such as adverbs, adjectives, "telling" language, and pleasantries between characters. Hone your sentences. Strive for clarity and beauty.
3. Add a "push-pull" energy of tension to any dialogue or interaction between characters.

MOVE IT

With notebook in hand, take a short stroll to a place near or in your workplace, neighborhood, or backyard. Pick an area of interest and stop to look at it (a sculpture, an old sign, a gnarled tree, a patch of graffiti). Write down some things you notice about it. Repeat this exercise on your next break. What new things do you notice? Write these down, too. Then find a way to use some of the details in a piece of writing, if possible.

PERSISTENCE IS PERSONAL
Ruthless Revision
by Lynn Carthage, author of *Haunted: Book One*, the Arnaud Legacy series

I can be a ruthless reviser, someone willing to throw out literally hundreds of pages— but I save them all in a computer file, in case I change my mind or find another project to use them for. I can even find exhilaration in wielding my scythe like a not-so-grim reaper. My neo-Gothic thriller, *Haunted,* the first in the Arnaud Legacy series (Kensington Books, 2015), provides a good example of how I kept working through problems in my novel until I came up with a marketable book. At first my teen girl protagonist, Phoebe, had a twin sister. They argued and were competitive, but it occurred to me that it is far more frightening to face supernatural terrors on your own. So I dumped the twin, and that also opened up the storyline for Phoebe to face issues deeper than struggling for identity against a sibling. I moved past the obvious to more fruitful, subtle trouble for her.

In an early draft, Phoebe learns information from an elderly librarian. I very much liked this character (and retain much fondness for him; maybe he'll show up somewhere else), but he wasn't injecting enough youthful vitality into my young adult novel. I transformed him into a gay male teenager, completely rewriting scenes and dialogue throughout the book to fit this new identity. But it still didn't feel right. I reread the book and paid attention to a character briefly mentioned offscreen, a female servant. Boom! She became this important side character—and this tactical decision also affected the plot in ways I couldn't have foreseen.

The way the book ends has been altered so many times that I'm not even sure now how it originally ended. I kept at it, trying new scenarios until I finally hit the one that felt right. One thing I tell creative writing students is to listen to that little uncomfortable voice in your head that tells you when something isn't working. It's easy to ignore, but if you listen, you will almost always push through to a revision that makes that voice cheer and then stop complaining.

Part Three
PERSIST

chapter 15

CONSIDER NO EFFORT WASTED

"A long apprenticeship is the most logical way to success. The only alternative is overnight stardom, but I can't give you a formula for that."
—CHET ATKINS

Please believe that my feet are firmly planted on the earth when I tell you the following, because I have seen the evidence: Everything you do for your writing practice counts toward future success. Every single bit. Every free gig, volunteer effort, labor of love, writing conference, or great idea that didn't fully pan out; all the hours and materials you donate; those paid, but especially those unpaid, events; every person you help or take advice from—all of it flows into the well of your success.

In fact, I hope you will begin, from here on out, to chart, count, take note of, and express joy and gratitude for all the opportunities you get to deepen your writing practice, because your practice is essential. It is the bedrock to any writing "career" you hope to have. It will feed you through all the low, dark, uncertain times, and it will always, always be there for you. But it needs your full commitment.

A writing practice is built on more than just writing. Doing the writing is the foundation, of course, but there are so many more avenues that add depth, merit, credentials, experience, collaboration, and inspiration to your practice. These connections form a web, and you never know when one strand of the web will connect you to another in a way that makes all the difference.

APPRENTICESHIP

I've peppered this book with the word *apprenticeship*, and this chapter is an ideal place to explore it further. The origins of apprenticeship can be traced back to the beginning of human history. Before schools and universities, long before computers and the Internet, people learned a trade or a craft by working with a master. You probably didn't earn much money, but by the end of your time of diligent hard work, you had a skill that could be used to make a living.

This same spirit was popular among visual artists, and it's how young, budding painters and sculptors learned the art.

I believe in a more modern version of apprenticeship to your craft of writing: That is, you learn it by doing it, by reading, by taking courses with talented writers, and by analyzing and practicing the very art you wish to excel at. Practicing is a skill we see so little of in this day of digital publishing and instant gratification, and one that should be a staple in your writer's tool belt. Want to write great novels? Read them, and practice writing them.

Therefore, practice is at the root of what I mean by "consider no effort wasted." Every trial, every experiment, every page of prose you set down is part of your apprenticeship to the craft that will bolster you throughout your life, if you tend it.

ADD IT UP

Below is a list. On a separate sheet of paper or on your computer, write down each of the items on this list that you have participated in or accomplished. And if you've done other items, add them, too.

- written or edited press releases as a volunteer or for money
- written articles as a freelancer or as a volunteer
- written or edited newsletters for organizations, schools, clubs, and groups you are or were a part of
- written or edited for a literary journal at a school or somewhere else
- acted as "secretary" for any group meeting
- written or edited a business plan or proposal for yourself or another
- written or edited a book proposal for yourself or another
- generated marketing materials, ad copy, or brochures for yourself or another
- edited other people's manuscripts or schoolwork: papers, theses, or dissertations
- written or edited content for websites for yourself or another
- attended a literary "salon" or "open mic" session where you listened to readers or read your work
- attended a literary or author reading at a bookstore, university, or theater
- attended any writing classes, through a small local arts organization, at a person's house, or through a university
- spoken at a meeting, group, or class as a volunteer or for money
- taught at a meeting, group, or class as a volunteer or for money
- attended a writing conference
- are or have been a part of a writers' group
- are or have been a part of Toastmasters or other speech clubs
- served as an event organizer

Some of the items you've listed have already borne fruit in your life. Maybe the newsletter you wrote for your son's school led to a paid gig for an organization that needs a newsletter. Maybe someone you met in that quirky lady's living room–based poetry workshop has gone on to be your best critique partner. Maybe that person you exchanged quips with at lunch at the writers conference turned out to be an agent who asked to see your work.

Many of these avenues haven't yet finished running their course or extending their usefulness in your life. If you stop taking your writing practice seriously, if you keep your work or yourself hidden, you may never know where they'll lead. If, on the other hand, you trust that these volunteer efforts, these opportunities to speak, teach, read, listen, and write, will eventually come to fruition, you'll be on the right track to building a lasting writing practice.

YOU DECIDE YOUR DREAMS

It's easy to be fooled into thinking there's a magic program, a specific path that only others know about, or a unique but mysterious road that you should take with a set number of steps to reach your dreams.

Nonsense. You decide when. You decided how.

You're the only one with the ability to follow through on your dreams. Only you know what you value, what you're willing to risk, and what your writing means to you.

Others may encourage you, support you, champion and cheerlead you, but they won't do the work for you.

If things haven't been going your way, or you can't see the fruit of your hard work yet, you may become convinced that you have bad luck, or that the odds are stacked against you, or that you're not talented enough. David Bayles and Ted Orland, the authors of one of my favorite books, *Art & Fear*, make the case that "talent may get someone off the starting blocks faster, but without a sense of direction or a goal to strive for, it won't count for much. The world is filled with people who were given great natural gifts, sometimes conspicuously flashy gifts, yet never produce anything."

You change your luck, your lot, and your odds simply by deciding to change them. That's the best way I can explain what motivates any major effort or change in my life, from adding in exercise to releasing my writing into the world.

After I made a change and started taking myself seriously, friends and colleagues asked, "Why did you start now?" There's rarely any magic in it: You just say, "Today is the day to take myself more seriously." This enterprising spirit is from the "fake it 'til you make it" school of success that I have long adhered to, otherwise known as the "What have I got to lose by trying?" spirit of taking chances.

I've spoken before about my own struggles with balancing my writing practice with the other demands of life. After my son was born, I found myself sleep deprived and drained of my former prolific energy to work my butt off. Thus I experienced the illusion that doors had closed to me. That writing had dried up. That work flow had ceased. Actually I was the only one to shut any doors. I ran out of energy to give to those endeavors because I was a shell-shocked, first-time mom struggling to raise a baby. Well, that baby is now a somewhat independent little boy and only child. His independence has freed up energy that had burrowed underground.

As I spun closer to my most recent birthday in August, the question arose in my mind: Why not take my writing career more seriously? I had always imagined my Big Dreams coming true by the time I was thirty. And while several of those dreams were realized, my thirties have been a decade of steep learning curves and countless opportunities that have taught me that loving the journey is crucial to any success.

This birthday, I listened to the whispering voice inside me that said, "Go spend the day with yourself. Listen to what comes up." Rather than having lunch with friends or my husband, I took myself to the Mount Madonna Retreat Center, a beautiful pastoral center overlooking the

Santa Cruz Mountains. I spent the day writing, meditating, and walking through the forested grounds.

The frustrated voice in my head that had been telling me doors were closed and opportunities were lost suddenly gave way to a softer voice I could hear only when I became very quiet. It said: "Now is the time to turn your writing career around. Today is the day to start." And since that day I listened to the quiet voice of confidence, I've sold two books, and I've been published in *The New York Times*, *The Washington Post*, and other publications I've coveted for years, like *The Rumpus* and *Brain, Child*.

No one will do it for you, and while in some ways that may seem a scary enterprise, the truth is, we are made to give ourselves over to creative work and to keep at it. Our brains are "plastic," capable of continual reshaping and rewiring through new experiences and activities, both of which are necessary to ingenuity and creative thinking.

No effort you make toward your writing practice is wasted. That day at the retreat center, I reminded myself of this fact and reached for reasons why it was all worth it: because I find value in my writing life; because I want to show my son what it looks like to commit, stick with, and rise above what's hard; and because I've invested too much of myself for too long to not keep giving it everything.

I opened the door a crack, and all manner of surprising, exciting, new big career opportunities came barreling through.

Now again—this was *not magic*.

These opportunities arose from all of the seeds I'd planted, some recent, some ages ago. I followed up on connections I'd let flounder. I finished ideas I'd left undone. I collaborated. I took some chances. Most of all, I just said, "Today is as good a day as any."

I also looked back on the twenty years that I have been actively pursuing a writing life and building a writing practice and I saw:

No effort was wasted.

And the biggest marker of my success? Learning to love the journey.

Do something for your writing life *today*. It will count. I promise.

WORK IT

Brainstorm a list of all the unpaid, unseen, unrewarded hours you've invested in projects, people, and writing. These may be things that haven't "paid off" in your mind. When you're finished, look objectively at each item on the list. See if you can't come up with one "gift" each item on that list has given you. Even if the "gift" is something like "It made me realize I never want to do *that* for a living." or "I learned to get back up after a fall." Reward yourself for your hard work with chocolate, a movie, or something that makes you feel good.

MOVE IT

This is the only place in the book where I'm going to suggest you multitask. Take a walk and bring with you any handheld device that is capable of recording. (In this day and age, just about every phone has this capacity, and digital recorders are cheap—and a handy device for a writer to have.) As you walk, use the recording device to "write" aloud. That's right—see what happens when you combine your musings with movement. You might find it's a good way to brainstorm and that you can do this when you need a break from the computer but not your work, while still getting in some crucial exercise.

If you really want to go the distance, look into a mobile workstation, such as a treadmill desk, which combines a tiny amount of movement with standing and working, and is much kinder to the body than sitting.

Or, if you're into the spin bike—a stationary exercise bike—consider using that time to revise something. One of my best friends, who does a lot of local theater, learns her lines while riding the spin bike.

PERSISTENCE IS PERSONAL
Bringing Old Bones to Life
by Jennifer Haupt, *Psychology Today* blogger at *One True Thing* and
author of *Will You Be My Mother?*

During my twenty-five years as a working writer, I have cranked out brochures about widgets and portals, gone to Haiti and Africa on assignment, spent eight years and counting on a novel that may never be published, been pulled over for speeding while cursing out Oprah's magazine for killing my Haiti story, sold book proposals and buried a few in the bottom desk drawer marked "graveyard"...

Well, you get the picture.

Every one of these projects has been, if not strategic, at least a part of some broader plan. Marketing writing during Seattle's tech boom helped to fund my trip to Rwanda, where I found the core of my novel. Writing fiction has made me a more skilled and creative nonfiction writer. The Haiti story that never made it into *O, The Oprah Magazine* because there was no happy ending has served as a piece of a larger creative nonfiction book project with Shebooks.

It's the big picture that matters.

I've learned, over the years, to look at every opportunity as a piece of the whole. It's not just about the money but about how a book project, a magazine assignment, or a trip where I may not even find a story to sell fits into the vision I have for my writing life.

Funny thing about that creative nonfiction book I'm now joyfully working on: I found the bones of it in the bottom drawer graveyard. I just needed to do some more living—and writing—to bring it to life.

chapter 16

COMBAT CRITICISM, SEEK CRITIQUE

"It's easy to attack and destroy an act of creation. It's a lot more difficult to perform one."
—CHUCK PALAHNIUK

Writers are exquisitely sensitive creatures, tuned in to the tiniest shifts in the environment around them and the widest spectrum of emotion. Writers are people with The Big Array of antennae—open to and thin-skinned against the world and its weightiness. Negativity—especially the doubt, fear, and self-loathing that writers feel after receiving criticism—sinks and pulls with a powerful gravity. In order to handle the feedback that will make you a better writer (and toughen your skin along the way), it's helpful to hold a couple of things in mind when criticism rolls in. Specifically, the answers to the following questions:

- What excites and thrills you as a writer?
- Why do you write?
- What meaning do you derive from your work?

Keep the answers to these questions near, as a strong reminder that there's a reason to your writing rhythms, that you can't be thrown off so easily by a little feedback or personal opinion, and that you are even less swayed or shaken by input sent with a nasty intention.

Equally important is that you cultivate an attitude of "take nothing personally." Even when criticism is *aimed* at you, choose to see it as the problem of the person who criticized. Learn to separate feedback about your work from your worth and talent; critique delivered in the spirit of improvement is worth receiving, and you may just need to wait until you're ready to use it.

Also keep in mind whether you want to stay where you are or whether you would like to grow in new ways. Constructive criticism often cultivates us, nourishing our roots and encouraging us to bloom in ways we didn't think possible.

CRITICISM VERSUS CRITIQUE

At some point in the life of your writing practice, when you seek reasonable, thoughtful critique, *criticism's* cutting jaws will come after you instead. So let me help you make an important distinction: Criticism is personal opinion that has little or nothing to do with you. Critique is a well-reasoned, astute approach designed to help you improve your work. It is work-centered, not personal. If someone says, "I don't like the way you write," or "What you've written is stupid and pointless," that's criticism; it's subjective personal opinion. My answer to that sort of feedback is: "You can't please all the people all the time." Critique, on the other hand, might sound like this: "When you write in the passive voice, it slows down your sentences." Or "I feel that too many adjectives hamper your action." Or even "I'm having a difficult time connecting with your character."

Criticism takes issue with you or your style or subject in an unhelpful way; critique offers you strategies for improvement. Big difference. In fact, improvement is the key to helpful critique. Any feedback that is designed to strengthen your writing is a good thing. Any criticism that simply points out what the reviewer doesn't like without including any tips for fixing it can be put aside.

FEEDBACK IS NECESSARY TO GROWTH

No writer grows without feedback and change. It's the nature of the craft that you wear creative blinders when you write: At times, you can only see as far as the next sentence. Feedback is crucial to making sure the rough vision in your mind unspools for the reader in a way that successfully translates your ideas and takes the reader on a clear journey. After all, you want to be read and understood. To fully embrace feedback, you may have to release any attachment to being "perfect on demand."

Now, I'm not saying that receiving strategies for improvement will necessarily feel great. For one thing, if you thought you were done working on a piece, or if you were especially attached to something that others are suggesting you change, that kind of advice can hit a sore spot inside you. This is where you need to return to your vision, your Writer's Code, and your goals for your long-term writing practice. Remember that critique is designed to improve the work, not comment upon your talent or insult you personally.

Is your goal to write and produce quality material that reflects who you are and finds you an audience? Is your goal to produce material quickly to get it published as fast as possible? Neither answer is right or wrong, but your specific goal will determine how and when you seek critique, and I highly recommend you do. The trick is to find trustworthy people who can give you help without attacking, nitpicking, or insulting you. Finding a good critique partner or group is much like finding a therapist or a church—the individual or group has to fit right and has to offer that exquisite balance of being able to push you out of your comfort zone and still hold the rope for you as you leap.

If you're wondering how and where to find a critique group, there are two main ways to go about this: online and in person.

The Internet opens you to a wider variety and a further reach because you can join writing and critique groups with members from all around the world, unconstrained by physical geography. Rather than point you toward generic critique groups, I take a page (literally) from author Becky Levine's book, *The Writing & Critique Group Survival Guide*. She recommends you join the organization most closely linked to the genre or style you write in. Some suggestions of hers include:

- The Society of Children's Book Writers & Illustrators (SCBWI): www.SCBWI.org
- Sisters in Crime: www.SistersInCrime.org
- Horror Writers Association (HWA): www.Horror.org
- Romance Writers of America (RWA): www.RWANational.org
- The International Women's Writing Guild: www.IWWG.com
- California Writers Club: www.CalWriters.org

Nearly every state has an arts council or alliance website that provides links for writers of every conceivable genre.

Another possibility is to post a request to start a critique group at your local library, a university, a bookstore, a café, and even your workplace.

All you really need are like-minded people with an eye for detail. Levine's book offers a number of wonderful strategies for how to approach critiquing.

TAKE WHAT YOU NEED

Sometimes you'll get more critique than you know what to do with, and the amount of work waiting for you can threaten to crush your spirits. In that case, it's best to ask yourself what, specifically, you are ready to work on and what you *want* to work on, and focus on *only* the feedback that will help you accomplish it. Put the rest to the side.

Give yourself some distance from the work, too, and then come back and reread the feedback. Some of the most outrageous and painful critique I ever received, especially while completing my MFA program, I later discovered wasn't awful at all when I put it down and came back to it. When my stories were freshly written, all critique was too much. Anything from "I'm having trouble understanding why your character made this choice," to "Are you sure that's the right word?" was enough to get my emotional hackles up. I had to walk away. Walking away is preferable to letting your spirits sink because your work is too raw.

On that note, and I speak to this in chapter seventeen, "Stave Off Sabotage," be honest with yourself about why you're seeking critique. If you put your work out too soon, hoping to hear that it's "brilliant" or that you "shouldn't change a thing," there is a good chance you'll be disappointed. Learn to recognize your writing rhythms. Consider how long you might need between penning a fresh manuscript and freely floating it to someone for suggestions without wanting to curl up in a fetal ball afterwards. Is it a week? Is it a month? Is it more? Don't let the urgency to publish sabotage your progress.

GET SPECIFIC

One way to circumvent the pain of critique is to get ahead of the ball and ask for specifics when you put your work out there. Create a list of questions that will help facilitate a healthy revision. I usually ask my reader specific questions such as:

- Where do you get bored or lose focus?
- Where do my characters' behaviors feel inauthentic or implausible?
- Does the plot stretch credibility at any point?
- Did any plot events not make sense?
- When you were finished, did you feel left hanging or wanting in any way?

- Did you feel engaged emotionally with my characters and their story? If not, where and why?
- Did you understand my characters' motivation?
- Did my protagonist undergo a significant change that you can explain?
- Could you see the setting and my characters visually?
- What did you like about my characters?
- What did you feel worked well in revealing my plot?

This is just a starter kit of questions, but it gives you an idea. You may have a good sense of the weak areas in your story, and you should ask your readers if they see these weaknesses. I always recommend putting these questions at the end of the manuscript, however, so that you don't bias your readers.

Also, I've found that in composing this list of questions you'll realize you have a greater sense of what needs work than you may have had previously. And you'll empower yourself rather than feeling at the mercy of your reviewers. It's also helpful to your readers, who can then put some real care and thought into these specific areas if they aren't sure what you're looking for.

CREATE REMINDERS

When you've been the recipient of painful criticism or overwhelming critique, your mind is not likely to be the most trustworthy neighborhood to hang out in. In that state, you can't be expected to remember all the good things you know to be true about yourself and your writing. I am a big fan of pasting these reminders in easy-to-find locations. Whether you have quotes, acceptance letters, inspiration, or just reminders, they will help to keep your spirits up.

For instance, on my wall is a handwritten sign I made that says:

Grumpy?
- Exercise

- Write
- Eat
- Rest
- Breathe
- Meditate
- *Repeat*

I could easily swap out "Grumpy?" for "Feeling Criticized?" We all need rituals to coax our wounded animal out of the corner. And the wisdom of the survivors who've gone ahead of us can be immensely reassuring in a bumpy patch. In addition to my sign, I've also posted quotes from my favorite authors and spiritual teachers, acceptance e-mails, and collages about writing that I've made. One of my favorite quotes is: "Do no harm, but take no shit."

OFF THE LEDGE

Despite all of my tips, you may still find yourself in the path of a wave of criticism so powerful that it knocks aside your logical mind, pushes your strategies just out of reach, and makes you feel awful. It may bust down your protective doorways, kick aside your sentinels, and shove you out on the window ledge, dragging with it an entire chorus of negative voices. Believe me, I've been there. One of my writing buddies called this state of being "the ledge"—as in, I went to such a dark place that she felt as though she were on the ground floor of a building talking me off the ledge far above. And indeed, at the time, I felt so bleak, so confused, so fraudulent because I was failing to see what others saw and struggling to create something that pleased others that my muse was threatening to jump from that ledge and leave me forever.

Perhaps this is a rite of passage all writers need to experience. Because if you've never heard these lying, foul voices, you can't fully appreciate just how wrong they are and how worthy you and your writing really are. I just hope you don't have to linger there.

Your Creative Support Team is crucial during these "on the ledge" times, particularly if your team includes at least one person who's been there before. But if not, I've discovered several other powerful antidotes to try.

Patronize or Engage in Other Arts

In the darkest of my ledge-standing days, I have always taken great comfort in music, poetry, visual art, and sometimes even just arts and crafts. The muse will gladly turn tides if you give her a new avenue. Sometimes the dark feelings are a sign that you need a break. Writing is nothing if not powerfully emotional, able to stir up deep corners of your psyche, and it is intricately woven into many writers' senses of identity, purpose, and value. When it isn't working or it feels wrong, turning your energies elsewhere can be a powerful antidote.

When I get too close to the ledge, I make beaded jewelry. It proves to be a deeply satisfying process. For one thing, in just a few minutes, I can make something beautiful without asking for or receiving critique, or revising. I know lots of writers who also craft to distract themselves and just as many who find that the cure for their dark emotions is to pop in a movie, mosh around their living room, or read someone else's work.

Read

If reading someone else's writing doesn't reinforce your negative feelings, you might find that it frees up your own stuck places. Reading can remind you why you write, what you love about words and stories; it also tunes your inner ear to the poetry and power of language, plants images in your unconscious, and essentially feeds the writer tank inside you. I believe that all good writers must read. Reading is an aerobics class for your writer mind. I'm especially a fan of reading a genre or form I don't write in. I love to read memoir and poetry, two forms I rarely write, because they still provide the keen ecstasy of language but also push me out of the tar pit of my stuck fiction writer's mind.

Write a Rant

Just because the goal is to eliminate your feelings of discouragement and doubt doesn't mean you have to feel only happiness and light along the way. There's nothing like a good old-fashioned raging or sorrowful rant that no one but you will ever see. Write it out, and write yourself down off the ledge. If you do this, I highly recommend you do it with pen and paper—there's just something tactile and satisfying about jabbing a pen into the page, denting its surface with your feelings, the ink like blood being let from the harsh words.

Champion Another Writer

Remember chapter seven, "Seek to Serve"? Here's a great place to exercise that intention in a way that can help you at the same time. As difficult as it is to lick your own wounds, if you can find a way to turn around and help someone else or offer wisdom or support, you may find that your own pain recedes. I believe that kind acts and goodness dissolve pain. At the very least, record what you're going through in a journal so that it can be of use to others later, perhaps as a personal essay or a blog post.

Get Some Exercise

Sometimes negative feelings just get stuck in your body. You receive a piece of criticism—maybe someone doesn't like your style, reviews your book negatively on Amazon, or talks badly about you to another writer. The feelings conjured by this criticism might sit like heavy stones in your gut, pressing in against your lungs and making it tough to take a deep breath. You might feel tired or weighty, as though you're suddenly wearing three of those protective lead jackets you have to wear to get your dental x-rays.

Your feelings derive from and affect your body. So when you find yourself looking down over the black abyss, don't just sit there. Move your body. Some form of exercise—almost anything, really—can make all the difference.

Don't just take my advice, though. All available research, including a study done by Norwegian researchers in 2013, states that even moderate physical exercise shows quantifiable results for improving mood, ranging from anxiety to depression.

As author Jonathan Fields puts it in an article for *Fast Company*, "For artists, entrepreneurs, and any other driven creators, exercise is a powerful tool in the quest to help transform the persistent uncertainty, fear, and anxiety that accompanies the quest to create from a source of suffering into something less toxic, then potentially even into fuel."

BEWARE THE PERILS OF PRAISE

On the other end of criticism comes praise, and who doesn't like to hear how wonderful, talented, compelling, interesting, smart, valid, or poetic their writing is? Praise comes in like a sweet scent and leaves you feeling lifted, euphoric, even purposeful. But as Anne Bradstreet writes in her poem "Meditations Divine and Moral," "Sweet words are like honey, a little may refresh, but too much gluts the stomach."

To a writer, praise, just like any potentially addictive substance, is a dangerous virtue that must be watched closely and kept in check. Why shouldn't you just revel in these moments of pleasure when someone bestows value or approval upon you? You should appreciate praise the same way you appreciate your nose, hair, teeth, or other attributes you were born with; that is, praise is largely out of your control. For the writer, praise does not a writing practice make. A writing practice is deepened and fulfilled when *you* acknowledge your own value and worth.

Once you've had that hit of praise, it's very easy to seek it out, to depend on it as you proceed with your creative projects. It can become so necessary that any critique feels hollow and harsh, pushing you away from doing necessary work and instead toward finding flattery. And let me reassure you, if it's flattery you seek, someone will always be there to provide it, but it doesn't mean it's for your benefit.

You have to learn to praise yourself, to discover and hone your own strengths. That comes with practice. Eventually you'll know what comes naturally to you, what you stumble over, and you'll teach yourself to seek the feedback that will shore up your weak parts and to acknowledge yourself for what you've done well. Yes, that comes with time, but the purpose of a writing practice is not to start out an expert or a master but to become better and make new discoveries along the way.

Interestingly I've noticed that when people do their truest, most authentic work, the praise has a way of flowing in.

WORK IT

Pick a recent criticism you've received. Write a rant. Really go for it. No one ever needs to see this, so there's no need for censorship or careful language. Let it out. Rip the page with your pen. Bleed your pain dry.

Next, be your own kind mentor, receiving the rant. Write a gentle letter back to your ranting self, offering support and encouragement.

Then, if you've received a recent critique that left you feeling raw, after getting some necessary distance, try to look at it objectively. Identify whether the critique is asking for something you just can't deliver or whether it simply touches upon a feeling inside you, such as disappointment because you thought you were finished. Read the critique as if it were written to someone else. Can you find a point or a place of agreement? See if you can't take just one small piece of the feedback and run with it.

MOVE IT

Psychiatry and physiology have been coming to the same conclusions in recent research: that mild, moderate activity can improve people's moods. Even in extreme cases of clinical depression, the simple act of taking a walk on a daily basis can allow some patients to experience full or partial remission of symptoms. While receiving criticism may not count as a clinical pathology, the effect it has on you may share some similarities. So when you feel the bitter sting of criticism, make sure you get up and do something physical.

I highly recommend walking in a natural setting, if possible. If not, the very act of ambulating is still helpful. Gardening, dipping your toes in a nearby pond, or, if you're experiencing arctic weather, slapping on the snow gear to feel the cold wind on your skin, can all help.

PERSISTENCE IS PERSONAL
Critique Strengthens Your Work
by Therese Walsh, author of *The Moon Sisters* and
The Last Will of Moira Leahy

Show me a writer who hasn't received heaps of rejection and criticism, and I'll show you an unsuccessful writer.

Critique is what illuminates our weaknesses and allows us to shore them up so that we can present our art again—stronger this time. And again, we may be criticized, and again, we are given through that criticism a chance to create exceptional art.

It isn't easy to be vulnerable to critique—to put our work out there with hope that it will be digested the way we meant it to be, accepted without question for what it is, or labeled as "perfect." I remember my first experiences with critique and the disillusionment I felt when I realized I hadn't conveyed what I'd meant to convey or that a character wasn't seen as three-dimensional. But after a while, something I now call "gut sense" kicked in and told me when those criticisms were right, and how, if I made revisions based on those things, I'd end up with a work that was still my own but that better conveyed the message I'd intended.

That said, not all critique should lead a writer to make changes to his or her art. You will reach a point when a critique feels wrong, when your gut sense tells you, "Nope, not this time." My debut novel, *The Last Will of Moira Leahy*, was affected by a village of critique partners and other outside influences, including agents who ultimately rejected the work while imparting some golden nugget of advice. But after five years of work and revising my manuscript more times than I can count, I was given some advice by a rejecting agent that felt ... wrong. In a turn that surprised me more than anyone, I rejected the rejecting advice and submitted again to a different agent who then took on my novel and sold it to Random House in a two-book deal.

Gut sense. It's important.

When you feel discouraged by rejection, take some time—an hour, a day, a week—to consider *why*.

- Do you feel confused by the rejection? Ask questions to better understand the critique.
- Do you feel you may not be up for the revision? Writer fatigue is common. Rest up. Rethink. And when you're ready, know you'll be able to attack your work with fresh enthusiasm.
- Do you feel you'll never be finished, that you're on the writerly version of a treadmill with no *off* switch? Writing well takes (a long damn) time. Hold tight to this: Your efforts are very likely making your work stronger while making you a better writer.

Embrace rejection. Every time you receive critique, accept it as a gift. What you do with that gift is up to you. Use it. Or don't. Listen to your gut sense. Perfect it. That's important, because one day your gut sense will chime in to say, "You're done, Champ. Get your book out there. It's ready."

chapter 17

STAVE OFF SABOTAGE

"Having a low opinion of yourself is not 'modesty.' It's self-destruction. Holding your uniqueness in high regard is not 'egotism.' It's a necessary precondition to happiness and success."

—BOBBE SOMMER, FROM *PSYCHO-CYBERNETICS* WITH THE MAXWELL MALTZ FOUNDATION

I wish I could say that everyone you'll meet along your path will wish you well and want the best for your writing practice. I wish, also, that I could say you will always make choices for your highest good, take all opportunities, and make only forward steps, but, hey, we're all human.

As you travel your road, you'll encounter people who don't have your best interests at heart. And, at times, fear, anxiety, and uncertainty will cause you to turn down, turn away from, or even sabotage chances to do great things.

The good news is, in both cases, you can arm yourself with knowledge to fend it off, try again, and practice good habits that will assure you as clear and upward-moving a path as possible. A solid writing practice is flexible and resilient. It will survive all attempts at sabotage.

FEND OFF SABOTAGE BY OTHERS

Those who make a concerted effort to sabotage your success are most likely quite unhappy and unfulfilled, or feeling stuck in their own creative lives. Your talent and success, therefore, may represent a sign to them of where they want to be or where they should be but aren't yet. And rather than behaving like adults and working on their own writing practice, they turn to childish behaviors that, in the long run, don't do anyone any good.

Others may feel threatened by your success even if they already have achieved a measure of it, because they do not trust their own practice. But it's not your job to assuage other people's fears by holding yourself back.

I have a wonderful writing colleague, already many times published herself, who decided to experiment in writing romance fiction and to self-publish it. Romance is a genre, she reasoned, that sells itself without much need for author platform. She did her research, chose a subgenre to emulate, then studied it, deconstructed it, and wrote her own version of a romance story. She did exactly what the advice books tell you to do. One of the successful authors in the subgenre, despite at first offering friendly advice, felt threatened when she saw my friend's book becoming successful. And she behaved badly: She bad-mouthed my friend in public forums and drummed up animosity.

And guess what? This negative energy did very little to harm my friend's actual book sales (though it did make her feel bad for a while). But it made the other person look petty, jealous, and mean. It made the person appear to be stingy and greedy, as if the romantic fiction market were hers alone to write in. It looked bad for her, not for my friend.

Of course, it still stung my friend, but with the support of her Creative Support Team, she regained her confidence and moved on.

The most important strategy for dealing with sabotage is to take the path of least resistance. In most cases, the less you do the better. Saboteurs want reactions. They want to know they've gotten under your skin and riled you. The truth is, if you're walking a path of integrity and doing your own thing, in the long run there's very little that an act of sabotage can do to you.

Forms of sabotage include when others:

- talk or post negatively about you and your work.
- talk negatively to people in positions to make decisions about you and your work.
- make excessively negative reviews of your work.
- betray your confidence.
- show or share work you asked not to be shared.
- bully you (more on that in a moment).
- privately message you or e-mail you nasty comments about you or your work.

In the cases above, remember the following.

- **TAKE THE PATH OF LEAST RESISTANCE.** Don't show saboteurs that their nastiness has any effect on you unless it is to report them to an appropriate source. Don't give them anything to go on.
- **DO NO HARM.** Never fight sabotage with sabotage—use your Creative Support Team, your journal, and your friends to vent and rage, but keep negativity out of sight. Never take the low road—it only makes *you* look bad.
- **BLOCK THE SOURCE.** Remember that most forms of social media and Internet access allow you to block people so they can't see you and you can't see them. This is a very useful tool. Don't torture yourself by keeping negative people and their nasty energy where you can still be affected by it.

IDENTIFY BULLYING

In this digital age, in which anonymous people can leave nasty comments and reviews, and rally others to join in, a line exists which, once crossed, can transform negative feedback into bullying. Bullying, by definition, is when someone personally attacks you in an aggressive attempt to cause you, your work, your reputation, or your sources of income harm. When commentary goes beyond the work and is aimed in a threatening manner at you directly, attacking your character, your talent, your nature, or anything of the sort, it is no longer criticism—it's bullying.

Several cases have been widely reported in which authors have experienced bullying via Goodreads or Amazon reviews, or in online forums. Bullying is no joke, and it hurts just as much as it does when it's in person. It takes on an even more egregious quality when it threatens to affect your livelihood or professional reputation.

Here are some strategies to put in place should you encounter bullying.

- **ASSESS.** First, it's important to take a clear-eyed look at the source to determine if it's really bullying or just negative feedback—in other words, is someone intending malicious harm or just stating his or her opinion? If it's the latter, I invite you to imagine Bob Marley singing that famous line, "You can't please all the people all the time," and to revisit chapter sixteen, "Combat Criticism, Seek Critique" if necessary. But for now, it's not your job to make everyone like you or your work. It's your job to write what you need to write, to be authentic and adhere to your vision.

  A negative opinion might sound like, "This story really didn't excite me. It wasn't what I expected. I wish the characters had been better developed." In contrast, a bullying comment might sound like, "What idiot wrote this tripe? If you keep publishing this dreck I'm going to tell all my friends not to buy it." The latter is personal, threatening, and uncalled for.

- **REPORT.** If you have determined that the behavior or feedback you're receiving is indeed bullying, then you have every right to report the behavior to the people who run the website, class, magazine, or source where the bullying behavior is allowed to exist. Sometimes moderators and administrators haven't yet seen it, and most of the time they will be glad you brought it to their attention. Then, as I recommend earlier: block, block, block. There's a wonderful government website with resources and information in case you still aren't sure: www.stopbullying.gov.

- **RESIST REACTING.** Bullies love a fight; that's usually what they're after. In an attempt to soothe some unhappy part of themselves, bullies aim to make you feel worse. Don't give them any fuel.

- **RALLY YOUR TROOPS.** What I mean by this is to rally your Creative Support Team to your aid but not in an attack against the bully. Don't stoop. Take the high road. I like to believe that bullies are proof that your words are summoning emotion for someone and that you've written something evocative; this doesn't mean you need to put up with it.

SELF-SABOTAGE

It's often much easier for writers to pinpoint sabotage coming from others; when they sabotage themselves it may be harder to see or acknowledge.

I once took classes from a writer I admired with all my being. She was not yet well known (she taught her workshops out of the living room of her little cottage), but she was personable, authentic, and immensely talented. The snippets of her work that she read were outrageously good. One day, after an intensive, all-day writing workshop, she told us that the editor of a well-respected literary journal had invited her to send her next set of finished short stories. The editor was going to personally put them ahead of the slush pile and read them all, because my teacher was that talented.

With a wry smile, my teacher wrinkled her nose and said, "I don't know why I haven't done it yet."

I didn't know either, and it would be many years before I realized that for whatever reasons, my teacher was afraid. Despite having the admiration of a respected editor, she didn't believe her work was good enough. She preferred to teach others rather than pursue her own success. I believe that she was able to come right up on the edge of success but was terrified to cross over and face rejection.

Tragically this teacher of mine died at the terribly young age of fifty-one from aggressive cancer and never got the chance to submit her stories. I've always taken it as a lesson: Don't sabotage yourself, because you don't know how long you have. How wonderful it would have been for my teacher to have seen her words in print in her favorite literary magazines before her death.

Being a self-saboteur doesn't make you bad; it suggests that fear or anxiety is holding you back. And I have great empathy for that state, having sabotaged myself a time or ten, too.

In addition to giving in to fear, other forms of self-sabotage include:

- showing work before you're ready for critique.
- querying agents or editors before you're done.
- saying yes to opportunities and not following through.
- saying no to opportunities you are capable of.
- asking for an opinion from someone who doesn't read your genre or style.
- suffering from perfectionism (revisit chapter nine for a refresher).

If you're engaged in self-sabotage I guarantee it's for one of the many reasons this book addresses: fear of failure, fear of being a fraud, fear of the responsibility of being successful, or fear of being seen. As Frank

Herbert writes in his novel *Dune*, "Fear is the mind-killer. Fear is the little-death that brings total obliteration." It really is.

So what should you do when you feel yourself pulling back and away from success or rushing in too fast before you're ready, which both have the same effect?

- **IDENTIFY YOUR PREDOMINANT FEARS AND GOALS.** In a journal, or with a trusted friend or professional, you need to figure out what you're most afraid of. The fears won't go away by themselves.
- **SET CONCRETE GOALS.** Oftentimes sabotage comes from feeling overwhelmed. You don't know where to start, where to turn, or which project to work on. (Visit chapter twenty, "Fight the Funnel Effect," for more on this.) Overwhelm leads to sloppy decision making and rash actions. Setting concrete goals, then, will help you focus.
- **MEDITATE.** Whether you sit in silence or meditate via your journal, calm, quiet reflection without distraction is a powerful way to reveal truth that otherwise hides behind distractions.

WORK IT

Take an honest look at your writing career and ask yourself if a figure of sabotage is at work in your own life. Make two lists.

List 1: Write your top three writing goals or top three desires—whichever appeals to you more.

Here's an example.

1. Acquire an agent.
2. Publish my novel with a mainstream publisher.
3. Make an income from freelance writing projects.

List 2: Beside each item, list your top fear for why you have either held back from pursuing your goal or desire, or have sabotaged it.

1. Acquire an agent. **Fear: I don't know how to write a query letter.**
2. Publish novel with mainstream publisher. **Fear: I need an agent first.**
3. Make an income from freelance writing projects. **Fear: I'm afraid I won't make enough to survive.**

Realize that your fears are usually anxieties that can be solved with a more minor step or action. From the example, for instance, if you don't know how to write a query letter, several books, websites, and classes can teach you this skill in a heartbeat. Don't have an agent? Once you master that query, hundreds of agents are out there waiting for you to submit your work. And so on.

Break your bigger fear down into manageable bites and steps until you land on the step that you feel you can do. When you try to take on the biggest step that touches on an even bigger fear, chances are it will lead to sabotage.

MOVE IT

Saboteurs, both internal and external, want your silence and your complicity. When you're feeling the effects of sabotage or bullying, it's time to make some noise. In this chapter you're going to exercise your vocal chords.

I recommend you go to a place where you can be alone. Do one of the following: Shout at the top of your lungs or into a pillow as long as you comfortably can, or—my personal favorite—put on a favorite song and sing as loudly and as passionately as you can. Bellow the song at the top of your lungs; really put your whole body into it.

chapter 18

ALLEVIATE ENVY

"Envy is the art of counting the other fellow's blessings instead of your own."
—HAROLD COFFIN

In the life of your writing practice there will come a time when someone you know strikes gold in an area where you are working hard or where you aim to be. You'll happen upon a crowing Facebook status announcing a book deal or the halcyon announcement of agency representation or a self-published book hitting the bestseller list and the gremlins of envy may come and sit heavily upon your chest. And likewise, it may happen that you become successful in a way that some peer or colleague has a difficult time handling. Whatever the shade of envy, you will know its greenish tinge, and it will not be particularly pleasant whether it comes from you or at you.

It can be hard to believe that there is enough to go around. Enough success, enough ideas, enough jobs, enough readers. The experience of envy is derived from a fear of scarcity. Whatever its origins, it is a belief that if someone else has the success you're after, there is less to go around. But it isn't true.

If (or I should say when) you feel envious, I offer you a reframe: Envy is a signpost pointing you toward what you really want. As easy as it is to tumble down the slope of discouragement when a high school buddy or a member from your writing group announces that she just scored a two-book deal or finally signed with an agent, fixating on how this didn't happen for you is a waste of your energy. Keep the following in mind:

- Envy steals your energy.
- Scarcity of resources is a lie your ego perpetuates.
- There is more than enough to go around. The world won't suddenly run out of opportunity, audience members, or money.

But you don't get off the hook that easily—a writing practice demands not just hours and miles logged in words but patience and faith that you are called to write for a reason, as well as commitment to refine and polish your vision. If you start grumbling about how others have succeeded where you have not or wondering what they did to deserve it, you know that envy has successfully latched its fangs into you, at which point it's up to you to shake it free. (Hint: Call in your Creative Support Team. Still stuck? Take it into the physical realm. Move your body). You can either waste time being envious, or you can put more energy and polish into your work and trust in your timing (or even push yourself to work a little harder).

Think about the success that other writers have right now. Phone someone whose career you covet. I can think of a dozen writers I knew "way back when" before they ever published novels. I was a part of the Zoetrope Online Writer's Studio a decade ago, and almost all of my peers on the site at that time have since gone on not only to publish but to do so with acclaim. I have traditionally published friends whose books hung out on *The New York Times* bestseller list and self-published friends who have sold over twenty thousand copies of their books on their own. Can you feel that tingle, that singular pull of longing for what others have? It's deep and it's old, an instinct that rises like a toddler parsing out what is his and what belongs to others. It has very little to do with the present moment.

The people who are "more" successful than you aren't lucky, and they aren't charmed. They worked hard at their writing practice; they studied; they honed their craft and persisted. They set a vision for themselves and plugged away at it. The main difference between you and those whose writing lives you covet is time and work. You may just be in a different stage of the process.

Here are some questions to ask when envy comes slithering through the gate.

- What part of your friend's (or colleague's) recent success do you truly wish for yourself?
- Why do you want this success? Sometimes you think you want what your friend has, only to discover that you only desire a slender part of it and not the whole thing.
- What aspects of that success do you already have? Remember chapter fifteen, "Consider No Effort Wasted"? You may already have more than you think and may simply need a reminder.
- What next steps can you take toward having this success for yourself?

Remind yourself: *My writing practice is for the long haul. I let go of instant gratification in favor of something that is long-standing and deeply founded.*

TAKE THE PATH OF NO RESISTANCE

Eventually if you dedicate yourself to your writing practice and show commitment, you will see successes big and small. To outsiders, strangers, or colleagues, some of these successes may seem instantaneous or unearned. Others may think you didn't work very hard or were handed success in some easy way. And this may produce professional envy directed at you.

Likewise, writing can appear to be quite a competitive field with a set number of "slots" and too many writers to fill them. Those who fear scarcity will see themselves as competing with you in some mad dash to a finish line that only allows one victor. You may find yourself on the unwanted end of negativity or criticism that derives from this place of envy.

In psychology, when someone projects a negative quality or feeling onto you that has nothing to do with you, it's called "transference."

Here's an example. You and a fellow writer are both freelance writers in a regional area. You both land stories in some of the same publications. Eventually you might be getting work while your friend isn't. Suddenly your friend decides that you are a terrible writer, or accuses you of stealing an idea, or writes an unkind comment on a blog post of yours.

You may feel ashamed, guilty, or sick to your stomach. You may feel as though you've done something you need to make amends for. You may feel the need to launch a powerful defense and rally your troops.

Don't do anything.

If you know that you are being hit with the transference of envy, then you don't need to act. Taking the high road and not honoring negativity shows that you have nothing to hide. Eventually the person making the big nasty fuss will expose themselves or go away. Maybe you can even find a tiny node of compassion; we all experience envy sometimes. You can take notes on how *not* to act when you find yourself coveting someone else's success.

HOARDING KNOWLEDGE HELPS NO ONE

If you live in the United States, you've likely grown up with the idea of a free market, an economic system that urges you to be an entrepreneur who pulls yourself up by your bootstraps and "get yours" while you can. I know firsthand that it's incredibly difficult to free yourself of the impulse to hold onto the knowledge you've earned (it's *yours!*) and to not feel threatened by letting anyone else have it.

But hoarding your knowledge, skills, and talent can be a mistake, particularly for writers.

Why? Because anything a new writer needs to know he will learn eventually. If a writer comes to you asking for help and you turn him away because you think he needs to learn from the school of hard knocks, he'll remember you for that. I'm not saying you can individually give time to everyone, nor do I mean you should give away your unique content, but I'm betting you could write a great blog post or article about your publishing journey, your hard knocks, and the difficult lessons you've learned and give this advice to those in need.

More than that, can you honestly say that you got where you are without *any* help along the way? Did you have no champions, investors, or people who believed in you? Did no one give you a leg up with an agent or editor referral or reveal a secret back entrance to a publishing opportunity through a contact or writing group that you might not have found yourself?

In the past fifty years, writers have fostered a culture of competition that wasn't as dramatic. I'm not sure if the more contemporary sense of competition comes from MFA culture (I went through an MFA program and can say that competition was definitely rife) or from social media's effect on how we share information, or if it's just the nature of the beast. That is, when human beings perceive a limited number of slots for success, they don't want to give away intel or secrets that might elevate someone else above the pack—and ahead of themselves.

But here is what I've found over the twenty years I've actively pursued a writing career: Every time I've helped someone, it has repaid me in kind or more. Those writers have remembered me, recognized me, and even rewarded me. I did not provide the help with any expectation of a return favor, and yet it often benefited me in the end. One of the writers I invited to help me interview authors on my literary radio show later shared with me his contact at KQED radio when he began working for them. Another time, an aspiring freelance writer with whom I shared everything I knew about the gig went on to review my book for me on her popular blog, which boosted my sales.

And the people I was too stingy to help? They went on to be successful anyway but were left with a negative flavor about me, I'm sure. You have nothing to lose by helping others; you have far more to gain.

When you hew to your own vision and write by your own authentic code, you aren't in competition with anyone else; you're weaving your own tapestry. Anyone along the path with you is a collaborator, not a competitor. When you listen to the signs, you are given information about what is right for *you*, what avenues, paths, opportunities, and people align with your unique vision. Nobody stands in the way of that.

WANT WHAT YOU HAVE

Here's another truth about the success that others have: It always looks better in someone else's backyard. You think you want the same success only because you don't have it yet. I know writers who have earned a huge advance on a book, only to learn that, because their book did not "earn out" that advance with book sales, the publisher wouldn't consider their next books, and their careers stalled. I know writers who received three-book contracts only to find that by book two they'd lost interest in the series or their beloved editor left the publisher. The shining achievements in someone else's life always look great from a distance. That's not to say that other authors aren't living the high life. Ultimately it doesn't matter. Focusing on what others have is a form of procrastination or distraction from your own writing. You definitely won't reach your dreams by longing for what others have. You'll only get there through dedication to your own path.

Keep in mind that sometimes the path chooses you. When I finally decided I was going to make writing a lifelong pursuit, I was sure that my first published book would be a novel. Instead, I've made my career by penning books *about* writing as well as teaching and editing. I didn't set out on this path, but it found me anyway. I seem to be good at it, and my efforts have brought me clients and attention.

Want what you have and work hard on it with a sense of whimsy and joy. A writing practice doesn't always have to be so serious. Let it be playful; let it be lighthearted at times. Always keep your love for it at the surface to tide you through the rest.

WORK IT

If you're feeling envious, jot down the specific focus of your envy right now. For example: "My friend just scored a book deal with a big publisher."

Now ask yourself: What are five steps I need to take on the way to my own book deal?

1. Get feedback from Creative Support Team.
2. Revise my novel.
3. Buy that book on writing killer query letters.
4. Write a killer query letter.
5. Submit my book to agents and publishers.

Breaking these tasks into smaller ones creates a road map for yourself. Taking action helps alleviate the energy of envy.

MOVE IT

Today focus on your physical strength. In what way are you already strong? Do you have good swimmer's shoulders? Solid legs that stand all day? Well-muscled fingers from all that typing? Once you've isolated the strongest part of you, pick a form of exercise that allows you to feel the strength you already possess. If you have strong legs, take a hike through hilly terrain. If you already like yoga, try Bikram, known as "hot yoga." If you find you're already good at endurance, try doing some short, intense intervals like sprints. Focusing on your strength creates a positive feedback loop that makes you feel more inclined to be nice to your body. Plus, when you focus on any area of yourself that you like or feel good about, it pulls out the toxic energy of feelings like envy.

chapter 19

BE RESILIENT AFTER REJECTION

"Creative greats have the resilience and drive to not get beaten down by 'losing' at a creative challenge. Just like athletes, they have the tenacity to get up, dust themselves off and refuse to quit. This mindset of determination is key to the creative process."
—CHRISTOPHER BERGLAND, FROM *PSYCHOLOGY TODAY* BLOG, "THE ATHLETE'S WAY"

Let's not sugarcoat it: Rejection hurts. Sometimes it has the power to steal your breath, jamming a fist into that tender part of your creative confidence. At its worst, it can convince you that you should give up—who were you to think that you knew what you were doing anyway?

So you may have to suspend disbelief when I tell you that rejection is an important part of cultivating a writing practice.

Rejection means that:

- you're putting yourself out there and taking risks.
- you believe in yourself enough to send your work into the world.
- you're making a statement that you take your writing seriously.
- you've taken an action that can help improve your work.

- you may have simply caught an editor or agent on a bad or an off day.
- you haven't found the right niche.

Remember, if you can change the way you view rejection, you'll fight off discouragement and put your energy where it needs to go: into your writing practice.

STAGES OF REJECTION

Like grief, I find that writers go through "stages" of rejection, and it's helpful to know which stage you are experiencing so that you know there's an end in sight.

1. **STING:** You feel the initial painful shock upon first receiving the rejection, and you're in a dazed state. Your hopes have been crushed.
2. **SHAME:** You feel embarrassed and exposed. "I must have done something wrong. I'm a bad writer."
3. **DISCOURAGEMENT:** Your shame leads to feelings of disappointment—in yourself and your writing. "I should just give up. No one is ever going to publish my work."
4. **INACTION:** You stop writing or revising your current project. "What's the point, anyway?"
5. **INERTIA:** Your fallow period becomes a habit, and you stop writing at all. "It's been so long since I've written something; I'm out of practice. Plus, I can't face being rejected again."

At some point every writer is faced with a choice: either to let the rejection continue its lethargic hold on your writing life—inviting inertia to take over—or to seek inner resilience to spring back. The writer with a writing practice sees rejection as a hash mark on the wall of the cell: another attempt at success made but not a reason to give up. The writer who believes in overnight success or instant gratification will feel these setbacks most keenly and struggle to overcome.

Don't be that writer. Be the resilient writer.

BE RESILIENT

Resilience is the ability to bounce back after rejection and is the opposite of inertia. Like everything else related to the craft of writing, it can be learned and strengthened through practice.

The first stage of becoming resilient is embracing rejection. I know writers who've wallpapered their offices with rejection letters, writers who've framed their first rejection letter, writers who have used a rejection as motivation to get back in the game. These writers have learned to be resilient.

You can see rejection as a message that encourages you to take action in one of two key ways: Go deeper, or go elsewhere.

Go Deeper

Often rejection is an exhortation to take your work deeper, to do more. You have to learn to step off the "good-bad" axis when judging the merit of your work. If someone rejects your work, that doesn't make it "all bad." It doesn't make you a bad writer, either. But it may mean that you need to refine, focus, or fix a specific part of your work. Why? Because writing is a craft, and your writing practice is the act of improving your craft through practice, polish, and persistence.

Europe has a long history of apprenticeship in the arts. Music, theater, and literature were all so valued that artists could obtain a "patron" who paid the artist solely to make his art. Over time this attitude toward apprenticeship has morphed into a culture of respect for the process of art making that acknowledges that no success happens overnight.

Here in the States, we like the arts, too. But, perhaps thanks to Hollywood and entertainment culture (oh yeah, and capitalism), art is more often linked to profit. That's largely why the independent or "indie" movement has risen in prominence in nearly every art form. Indie music, indie moviemakers, and indie authors are people who have all said, at one point or another, that what they create isn't just about money—it's also about love and purpose and creative control.

As long as you subscribe to perfectionism or instant gratification, or are driven only by making money, you will feel the sting of rejection far more than your compadres who shrug it off and then return to their deeper reasons for making art, such as expression, joy, and connecting to others through words.

Go Elsewhere

There are hundreds, even thousands, of sources where you may decide to submit your work. Between literary agents, literary magazines, small publishers, and other online markets, where you choose to submit your work may still only represent your best guess, even if you do thorough research. This means that, inevitably, you'll sometimes pick the "wrong" place. The decision of whether your work "belongs" in a certain publication or is "worthy enough" for literary representation contains a huge element of subjectivity. Don't ever forget that every agent, every editor at a publishing house or literary magazine, is just one person. While she is certainly representative of a tone, a style, or a brand of writing, she is still but one filter your work passes through. To be rejected, therefore, may simply mean that you submitted to the *wrong-for-you* place.

If you feel you've gone deeper, if you know that you've achieved your vision and honed your craft, then there's no reason to stop after a rejection—or several. You just need to pick up and keep moving.

SEEK VALUE

It's a lot easier to bounce back from rejection if you set up your writing practice to reap some reward that has nothing to do with the approval or praise of others. In other words, when you determine what value your writing has for you, you become less susceptible to the gamut of feelings that rejection can bring.

How do you do this? Ask yourself: How do I feel when I write? What does writing do for me? What do I give others through my writing? Most writers I know feel something between the euphoria of a good glass of wine and the endorphins of a runner's high after writing. And that's not just when "inspiration strikes" but even after you've sat blinking at a white screen for two-thirds of your writing session. I know people who struggle to express their feelings verbally until they've committed them to ink or pixel on the page and others for whom writing snippets of story ideas during the day at work is enough to hold them over until later writing sessions. Writers write, right? Even if you write for income or to promote your cause, you write for the deeper meaning or reward that writing brings.

The Myth of Overnight Success

Most famous writers are known for a "breakout" book; while this was the author's first *published* book, it might actually have been the third or ninth or *twentieth* novel the author had written before success came to perch on the windowsill. My friend Caroline Leavitt, author of such best-selling literary novels as *Is This Tomorrow*, *Pictures of You*, and seven other books, experienced a series of mishaps in her early years of publishing that nearly made her give up hope of ever publishing a successful book that would launch her writing career. And then she found her current agent, who took her work to the small publisher Algonquin Books and turned Leavitt's novel *Pictures of You* into a bestseller, changing the direction of her publishing career.

Or take the story of Kathryn Stockett, whose novel *The Help* hit the *New York Times* bestseller list in its first week of publication and spawned a movie starring Emma Stone and Viola Davis. Her manuscript received sixty rejections from agents before number sixty-one accepted her and sold her novel to Amy Einhorn Books. This is all to say that if your first book doesn't make magic, I beseech you, by the mother of all holy things, keep writing! And even if you get sixty agent rejections, keep at it.

The moral of the story is: Overnight success comes after walking a road over time of practice and determination. No effort is ever wasted as a writer; you've just walked another step in another mile in your writing life. Anything else is rushing, and you know what your mother taught you about what haste makes ...

The Numbers Game

When writers are given advice on rejection, they're often told they need to "get over it" and "toughen up." I don't actually want you to become so tough, however, that you become jaded and grumpy, which can lead to creative block and far too much time spent "on the ledge."

What you *can* do is think statistically. Submitting and publishing is ultimately a numbers game, and you have to play that numbers game in order to be published in mainstream venues (and frankly, even to be self-published—you still have to find an audience to sell to, and that's often a trial-and-error process). Tell yourself, *Okay, that's rejection number five, which means I'm in the game, baby, but nowhere near done!* In the end, the more you submit, the greater your chances for acceptance. So you can train your mind to see those rejections as greasing the way for future acceptances. The only surefire way to avoid rejection is to never submit your work—in essence, giving up on your dream, and you're not about to do that. Your life would be dull without your writing, after all.

Fail Up

I don't know too many people who stand up proudly and shout for joy when they experience a failure, whether they are accused of doing something wrong or poorly, or a creative experiment doesn't go the way they'd hoped (or a thousand other examples). When you "fail," the more people who are aware of it, the more you may want to burrow away in a dimly lit cave until all memory of it has passed.

But what if I told you that you should celebrate and share your failures? That failures are signs of experimentation and creativity, of stretching and pushing yourself bravely toward the unknown?

The kind of failure I'm talking about is the result of attempting something big, new, or challenging that doesn't go as you planned. And with all creativity, attempts are required, and "failures" are inevitable.

Stop trying to hide your failures.

Fail publicly, and often.

When I teach a writing class, I always ask my students to share their struggles in the public forum. What's hard for one person often strikes a chord of another. When a student shares one of her failures, a new understanding is created, and she sees that it's okay to be viewed as imperfect or inexpert. For instance, one of the students in my plot class once shared her frustration that her novels always sagged or grew boring in the middle. Another student in the class pointed out that she had a tendency to make things easier for her character, rather than more difficult, and that doing so diminished tension and drama. It was an epiphany for her that changed her writing process. Often an outside-the-box answer from a fellow student offers more insight than I alone could give them. I come with a limited set of experiences and knowledge, whereas my students, who range in ages and backgrounds, can provide information I can't. Once, for example, a student who worked as a nurse was able to correct inaccurate details about another student's character's hip surgery. Another time, a younger student gave an older student tips on how twentysomethings really talk.

There's vulnerability in admitting to your imperfections and your gaps in knowledge, which in turn allows others to connect with you on a deeper level. Think of those times you saw a stoic parent collapse into tears over his child's illness or the moment someone you love revealed painful wounds you didn't know were bleeding behind the scenes. That sort of vulnerability brings us closer together.

I did an internship at a bodywork institute in my twenties when I was pursuing massage therapy as a temporary career. My teacher always used to say, "I highly recommend you fail in public and as often as possible." He meant that as long as your individual ego is attached to the mantra "I'm bad and wrong," your growth and change are limited. But the moment you stand before others, laid bare and uncertain, the story changes. Others often express compassion and empathy, and solutions that you couldn't have dreamed up alone flow toward you.

Failure seems a patently American quality—we of the entrepreneurial mind-set, of the bootstraps that must be pulled up alone, of the iconic image of the rugged individual. We're fed subtle messages of doubt: that if you don't do it yourself, alone, and correctly or perfectly the first time, how will you succeed?

You'll succeed the way that artists and innovators have for centuries, by learning from your "failures." You will begin, in essence, to "fail up"—a concept defined by New York University psychologist Scott Barry Kaufman about resilience in the face of failure. To fail up means to see what doesn't work as a lesson to learn from, not a reason to whip yourself into a shame corner. It means you understand that there is both great wisdom and necessary humility in letting others see you learn from your failures.

More important, when you admit to your failures, you discover several key things: that your failures are more universal than you thought, that others have compassion for your errors, that there is room for improvement, and, ultimately, that failure opens the door to greater, deeper, and more honest connections with others.

WORK IT

If you have a rejection letter of some kind, pull it out and read it. Or imagine the letter you are afraid to get if you haven't yet received one. Now, write a short note to the person who sent you the letter (not to be sent).

"Thank you for rejecting this [story/novel/idea]. It made me realize that I need to go elsewhere/deeper. It allowed me to figure out: _____ _____."

And sometimes a little humor helps. A friend of mine and I both received what we felt were fairly harsh rejections from the same editor of a coveted publication. Comparing letters, however, we decided this editor simply had a blunt style. To vent our feelings, we wrote our own absurdly harsh letters in the voice of the editor to fictional rejection recipients to make ourselves laugh. We were surprised by how much better we felt afterward.

MOVE IT

Since rejection has a way of weighing down the body, sometimes you need to assertively move that feeling out of yourself. If your physical health allows, do one of the following things.

- Hit tennis balls with a racket, or a handball with your hand, as hard as you can against a wall for ten to fifteen minutes.
- Run a really fast sprint down the street, as hard as you can.
- Beat a pillow. Really. It feels so good. Pound your fists into it. Shout. Imagine you're releasing all that negativity with each pound.

PERSISTENCE IS PERSONAL
Going Small to Make It Big
by Jessica Inclan, author of *How to Bake a Man*, *Her Daughter's Eyes*,
and other books

A story I wrote twenty-one years ago was published in December 2013 in a literary journal. It's hard to believe that I not only remembered this short story existed but that I was able to dig it up in my hard drive, buried as it was beneath layers of computer portals and folders.

But when I read the call for stories about loss, well, my mind flashed to this story I had written about a woman thinking about her life as she watches her youngest daughter die.

I dug around (*click, click, click*, voilà!), opened the file, and went at it with an editor's eye. And it was accepted, over two decades after I'd started it.

I'm not one to give up. Well, maybe there are hours of despair ... for instance, the time I got twelve rejections in a row, in one hour. (Have you ever made the connection between holiday weekends and rejections? Editors are at home, too, and they get back to you really quickly.) And I felt pretty bad when my second agent fired me via e-mail. ("It's not me, it's you"). I also thought about throwing in the keyboard when my third agent was unable to sell the YA novel I revised many times (during the course of countless revisions, the setting changed from the year 1977 to 2184!)—especially when the novel almost sold twice. But, no dice.

And there was the time I worked on a novel with my second agent for a while—and that might have been what made him want to dump me. Take note when agents pass you over to their assistants. In any case, I left that relationship with a novel draft of a story I really loved.

So recently, when I read about a very small publisher who wanted novel manuscripts, I decided to dust off my story about a young woman who decides to quit business school and start her own baking company. I thought, *What the heck?* A few weeks later, I received the e-mail stating they would love to publish the novel: a small print run and a digital edition. This isn't the mega contract of my grasping dreams, but it is an acknowledgment of my work and persistence. And more important, it's a testament to my stubborn nature and penchant for closure. Eight years later, my story is almost ready to launch into the world.

My advice about this writing business is to remember it is a business. What wasn't working twenty-one years ago may work now. What didn't work in 2008 might work in 2015. The market shifts. Tastes change. The best news? I'm a better writer now than before. I can fix things I didn't know were broken all those years ago. My writing practice combined with my refusal to give up has helped me assess my own work.

My last bit of advice is about your hard drive: Make sure you save all of your documents. And label them better than I did. It will save you a lot of clicking.

I just might see who wants a novel set in 2184. Or maybe I need to wait twenty years. Trust me, I can do it.

chapter 20

FIGHT THE
FUNNEL EFFECT

"There are too many ideas and things and people. Too many directions to go. I was starting to believe the reason it matters to care passionately about something is that it whittles the world down to a more manageable size."
—CHARLIE KAUFMAN

On the other end of writer's block, which is often caused by a feeling of lack or emptiness, is something I call the "funnel effect." This occurs when too many ideas are trying to force their way down the chute of your mind, leading to overwhelm—and then, sometimes, to paralysis. How do you choose between the novel that is begging you to write it, the nonfiction book you think might make a mint, and the short stories you can submit for publication more quickly?

Your projects are your children, but they're children that don't always get along. You can't give them all your attention at once; you have to set aside separate times to attend to each of them. Remember when I talked about the myth of multitasking in chapter four, "Tame Time"? Your ego, driven by the illusion of big, bold, flashy success, will try to convince you that not only can you work on all of your projects at once, *you must* in order to secure your day in the spotlight.

You can't write everything all at once, just as you can't please all the people all the time.

You have to choose.

My experience is that you have the mental capacity for a maximum of two writing projects at any given time, especially when those projects are different from one another. Ideally you would devote your attention to only one project at a time. If you think you're going to simply carve out five little time slots in a day to work on five projects, I'll tell you what the result is likely to be: five unfinished projects driving you crazy and creating more of the same frustration that drove you to read this chapter in the first place.

As I said in chapter nine, finishing something frees up mental space. And dividing up your projects over different times of the day is not going to fool your subconscious. Instead you will carry the sum total of all the projects you're trying to work on in your mind at once, and doing so will add up to feeling overwhelmed. "Overwhelm" (it's not really a noun, but for the purposes of simplicity, let's use it) leads to paralysis. Paralysis leads to discouragement and negative self-talk focused on how you are not capable, talented, or productive (all lies).

LOOK FOR THE SPARK

Knowledge is really only a fraction of the battle when it comes to overwhelm; you still need to take action. So you have multiple projects vying for your attention, but you can't choose them all. Where do you start?

Go where there's electricity.

Let's say you went on two different blind dates. Both dates went well, and you were left with a good impression of both. If you asked me, "Which one do I choose for a second date?" I'd say: Which one gave you the best, most alive feeling when you were together? Which one made you lose track of time, bypassed your self-consciousness, or made you laugh? These same qualities apply to your writing projects. Which one turns on the synapses, engages the mind and the heart, excites you when you begin to work on it? If you're working at something purely out of a feeling of obligation, put it aside and come back to it later. You might begin a project for a hundred different reasons: It seems timely, it haunts you, you're trying to finish something you started, it's a "hot topic," or the like. But those reasons are not as motivating as the white-hot feeling of commitment that comes with the right project—the one that simply calls to you with ferocity.

If all of your projects are calling to you with the *same* amount of intensity—no voice is shouting louder than the others—then pick the one that is (a) closest to being done or (b) most likely to get finished. You need to get the near-finished project off your plate and out of your head before the feeling of overwhelm can go away completely. Other times it may be best to pick the shortest project or the project you know will be easiest to execute and therefore will be done quickest.

This is my system for how to pick and choose when too many projects vie for my attention. Choose from one of the following.

1. Pick the most exciting, fun, electrifying project (even if it's not practical). This will create positive energy that will carry over when you must spend time doing your writing "chores," such as revising, writing query letters, researching agents, or other less pleasurable writing-related activities.

2. Pick the most pressing project, due to a looming deadline or commitment or other urgent reasons. If you're choosing between projects that have no due dates, skip to number 3.

3. Pick the most "persistent" project—the one that sticks in your skin and won't be ignored even though it's not necessarily the one you planned on writing.

AVOID PARALYSIS: START SOMEWHERE, ANYWHERE

The truth is, it almost doesn't matter what project you work on as long as you work on something. The worst feeling is to find yourself paralyzed, at your computer, unable to start anything for fear of picking the wrong thing. This state of paralysis is sadly not uncommon to creative types, especially if you're choosing between writing that will bring you pleasure and writing or doing other work that is due to an audience. This is why I return to my earlier advice: Do your favorite writing first, as soon as possible. That way, you've already gotten it done and can't beat yourself up or waste energy feeling guilty that you didn't get around to it. For me, this is always my fiction versus the freelance articles on my plate or the essays I write to explore personal subjects directly.

Just make sure you choose *something*. Do eeny-meenie-miney-mo if you must; there need not be a science to choosing.

PREVENT PROMISCUOUS PROJECTS

I know how it goes: You're hard at work on a big project when you hit a snag and find yourself deep in the tangles of something you can't easily tease out. For many novelists, for instance, the middle of a book poses a very specific kind of threat: plots sag, characters lose their motivation, and writer's block threatens to take over. (They don't call it the "muddy middle" for nothing.) And while you're busy railing at your unmotivated characters or your blocked muse, it happens: You see the glimmer of a very sexy new idea just off the horizon. Perhaps the new idea is shorter than what you're working on or more "timely." So you traipse off after the lure of its siren call, thoroughly seduced. For a while. Until, inevitably, you find yourself in exactly the same place as you were with the other project.

If you keep up this habit of abandoning one project in pursuit of another, you'll eventually have many unfinished projects and a lingering feeling of dissatisfaction because you never finish anything. As I've said before, unfinished projects take up an awful lot of mental energy and prevent you from moving forward. A lack of completion can lead to negative voices that suggest you are a "fraud" and a "disappointment," and create a cycle that's very hard to break.

And all of this will add up to a new glut of half-finished projects that vie for your attention, pull on your guilt, and provoke that dead-end feeling.

You've probably heard of Malcolm Gladwell, author of *Blink* and *Outliers*. He asserts that any great work of art requires "ten thousand hours" before you can call yourself an expert. At first glance that figure probably sounds daunting, but he's talking about *all* the hours that go into your practice—the hours you spend learning, practicing, and getting back up after your mistakes. The "work" you do as a writer is not like the work you do performing data entry or stocking shelves—work that fills a need but doesn't build upon itself. Writing is cumulative, aggregate: The more you do it, the better you get at doing it, the more you learn, and the deeper both the work and the practice become. Therefore, you'll experience many moments in your writing practice where the work required of you feels difficult and is perhaps harder than what came before. You may not want to face it. Wouldn't it be so much easier if someone just told you that your work was done, the story was perfect, and you could just press on? But what's the point in that? If you could turn out perfect work all the time, how would that shape you or encourage you to grow?

This is a long way of saying: When the writing road gets rocky, when the project seems to mock you and defy your understanding, don't just start something new. Instead, persist. Keep at it. Be one of those writers who gives your most concerted, passionate effort. You will not only produce better work, but you will feel proud and unencumbered of those many floating projects, and you will avoid the feelings of overwhelm brought on by the funnel effect.

TAKE A DEEP BREATH

I, too, live in the modern world of two-income households, in which the pace of life feels hectic, scattered, and urgent. How often have you had to schedule time to see your spouse, not to mention your friends, or were only able to let your shoulders relax on Saturday morning for the first time all week?

Stop for a moment. Take a big deep breath right now.

I know how busy life is. I know how many demands are upon you. I know how easy it is it put off the thing you love for a "later date" because you envision having time in the future—just not right now.

And I know that "later date" may never come if that's where you put your dreams.

No writer for whom writing is even the least bit important ever regrets writing. It's not something you would give back or trade for something else. Studies have shown that at the end of life, dying patients report regrets over *not* pursuing those dreams.

So, yes, your life may be hectic and overwhelming, but I promise you there are a few small fissures of relief inside that funnel that you can carve out for your writing. And once you begin to carve them out, they have a funny way of widening and multiplying.

If you're not sure where to look for spare time, return to chapter four and read the section on how to carve out distractions.

WORK IT

Is your needle totally stuck on overwhelmed? Write the names of your many projects on slips of paper, and put them in a hat or basket. Pick one. Commit to whatever you choose, and go for it.

MOVE IT

When you're overwhelmed, even the everyday tasks seem difficult. Shawn Achor, author of *The Happiness Advantage*, describes what he calls the twenty-second rule. If it takes you twenty more seconds to do one thing over another, you're likely to pick the activity that takes the lesser amount of effort and time, no matter what it is. If you want to learn the guitar, for example, and you keep it by your bed instead of in another room, you're more likely to pick it up in the morning. I think this also applies to physical exercise. I'm more likely to get down on my floor and do some yoga stretches at home if I have my own mat than I am to make it to a class at the gym across town. So right now, for your overwhelm movement break, focus on *micromovements*. In other words, move your body in small but meaningful ways.

- Close and open your eyes for five seconds each.
- Stretch each finger.
- Tilt your neck to one side, then the other.
- Lift or shake one leg, then the other.
- Sit in a comfortable spot and inhale deeply for five seconds. Then exhale slowly for five seconds. Slowing your breathing brings calm, which leads to better focus.

chapter 21

TROUNCE TABOO

•••

"Because this business of becoming conscious, of being a writer, is ultimately about asking yourself ... How alive am I willing to be?"

—ANNE LAMOTT, FROM *BIRD BY BIRD*

•••

•••

"Whenever a taboo is broken, something good happens, something vitalizing."

—HENRY MILLER

•••

The idea of taboo—a forbidden or scary subject—in writing is such an interesting concept. What may be taboo to me may be laughably no big deal to you. Each of us is shaped by a set of experiences in which certain topics are "allowed" or comfortable, accepted or not. And there are stories you may be burning to tell that cross a taboo line only because they reveal information about others, as well as stories that are tenderly vulnerable because they expose you personally. You may also want to tackle some topics in your fiction that you have a personal stake in and that take on culturally taboo or controversial subjects.

Just because subjects are taboo doesn't mean that you should not write about them. There's an art, literally, to writing about what challenges you and others—in fact I'd say that writing what is raw and real is one of the essential roles of the writer. Who else opens up these sealed spaces for others? If we hark back to Richard Bausch's quote in chapter eleven, "Be Bold, Write Bravely," then you might even say it is the duty, the responsibility, of writers to write about what other people cannot. By writing what is taboo for you, you act as ambassador for others who will never find the words.

Taboo challenges can make an activist out of many a writer. A good friend of mine became active in marriage equality campaigns on behalf of beloved friends and family members, and she used her writing to spread her message, even though it's a hot-button issue. Another friend of mine has used her considerable social media platform to write about her own childhood sexual abuse and has provided a forum for others to do so in the process. She's turned her pain, a formerly taboo topic in her family, into an outlet for a greater good.

ALCHEMY OF ART

In the gorgeous and painful memoir *Truth and Beauty*, which tells of Ann Patchett's friendship with the late writer Lucy Grealy, Patchett recounts Lucy answering an audience's questions after she'd given a reading. Grealy suffered from a childhood cancer of the jaw that led to disfiguring surgeries and a lifetime of struggle out of which she crafted a remarkable memoir.

An audience member asked, "How do you remember all those details?" And Lucy, noticeably annoyed by the question, is said to have answered, "I didn't remember it; I wrote it."

The point being she crafted her story as she wanted to tell it and turned it into art—provocative, powerful material that is designed to take the reader to places that real life might not actually provide in the moment of living.

Writers make art of experiences in order to both understand them and also to shed light and reveal truth. The hotter the topic, the more necessary for you to make your experience into artifact, that is, to do the work of the craft—to revise—so you can put distance between that which terrifies you and the reading public. When you *craft* your stories, rather than bleed them out onto the page, you turn them into something new, a bit removed from you, and reduce the sting of fear or shame. Then, you can also take pride in *how* your story is written, and *why*, rather than just focus on the raw nerve that's been exposed. This is just another reason why revision—honing your work to find just the right image, just the right structure, sentences, and tone—is so important. The point is not to push you into perfectionism but to urge you toward using the craft as a vehicle to write about the full spectrum of the human condition, from the beautiful to the horrifying.

Many writers will tell you that it took years to work up the nerve to write about certain subjects, while others will admit they were waiting for relatives to die before they could tell the truth. But as Anne Lamott so humorously reminds us in *Bird by Bird*: "You own everything that happened to you. Tell your stories. If people wanted you to write warmly about them, they should have behaved better."

Writers who tackle taboo subjects are the ones that bring us stories of the Holocaust, of the oppressed, the abused, and the silenced. In some countries it is taboo to criticize leaders or discuss the past, and writers ranging from Salman Rushdie to Orhan Pamuk to Malala Yousafzai have risked their lives or alienated family to write about these prohibited topics.

Some taboos are closer to home: tales of abuse and addiction, of poverty and racism, of single parenthood, and of choosing a different religion or political party or lover than one's family would like. There are taboos about revealing your parents' line of work or how little money they made, and there are taboos about discussing wealth, inheritance, or opulence in your family.

It almost doesn't matter what the taboo is, only that you identify these hot-button areas in your writing and then find a way inside them. That's right—I'm urging you to explore the taboos in your life rather than walk away from them. For one thing, these forbidden topics have a way of seeping up through the cracks if you don't let them in. They might even cripple your attempts at creativity because they want, or even need, to be written before you can move on to other territory.

CLAIM YOUR STORY

Not to sound depressing, but the news keeps rolling in that life is short. Okay, so maybe it's longer than our medieval ancestors', but in the aggregate: short. And the fact is, if you wait for someone to die, move, approve of, or validate you before you write your story, the chances are stacked against you already; people rarely do things on your schedule, especially if they don't know you're waiting, and most likely because they may not see things the way you do.

And they shouldn't. You have a singular perspective; it's no cliché. You are the only one with your particular vision and view. And you are also probably the worst judge of the value of your own material or whether your life is "interesting." You may think your stories are dull or already done or not good enough, but that is all just ego bluster. If you haven't noticed, the ego may be part of you, but it isn't always your friend. It's like an avaricious, mean-spirited, pesky little sibling that lives inside you and urges you to always be better than you are now—there isn't a lot of self-acceptance inherent in its structure. It's not all bad, of course—your ego also helps you survive in the world, and it gives you a fallback when you need to muster confidence. But you can't let it run the show. In other words, don't listen to it or any other voice that tells you that you can't write your story.

Your story belongs to you. It is your perspective, your version. You lived it. You own it. Just as no one can tell you that your feelings are wrong, your experience isn't wrong either. They may not agree with it or like it, but it's still your *experience*. It may be different from the experience of those who were with you, but it's yours. Memory is an unreliable witness anyway; science has shown that what we think of as ironclad memories are not only subjective but also change and fade over time. All anyone has is their version of experiences, and even if someone else thinks it's "wrong," no one can deny what you remember, because no one is inside your head.

This year, I've published more raw, personal essays than in the twenty years I've been actively publishing. Since these pieces tell about some of the hardest experiences of my childhood, including my mother's years struggling with addiction, I'm always a little nervous about how she'll feel. So it was gratifying when, after reading a recent piece, she texted me:

> Keep that cathartic narrative flowing. It's really helpful. All of us need perspective from outside ourselves. It's like my favorite quote from the Shawshank Redemption: You either have to get busy dying, or get busy living.

She then went on to remind me of what her former sponsor, Ruby, once said in her early days of sobriety: "The truth will set you free, but first it might make you throw up."

Ken Eisold, Ph.D., writes in a *Psychology Today* article in March, 2012: "… neuroscientists have shown that each time we remember something, we are reconstructing the event, reassembling it from traces throughout the brain … We could also say [memory] is adaptive, reshaping itself to accommodate the new situations we find ourselves facing. Either way, we have to face the fact that it is 'flexible.'"

To me, this position offers great freedom in recounting your experience through an artistic lens in a way that will make meaning out of experience. The specific facts may matter a whole lot less than the feelings and realizations they evoke.

I'm confident you'll find great power in writing about what once seemed taboo and giving it a new shape, a new understanding.

WRITE ABOUT OTHERS WITH COMPASSION

All that said, there will come a time when you do need to write about others, those people whose experiences you can't speak for, per se, except as a witness or to quote their words. Or you may be writing about them as they relate to you. I've found a couple of key tricks for writing about others in personal essay and memoir that, once again, allow you to tell your version of events.

As long as you write with the intent to explore a subject for the purpose of coming to greater understanding, rather than blaming, you can approach the material as it abuts other people's lives with care. Here are some methods for approaching personal material.

- **SEEK UNDERSTANDING.** Write about others and their stories as they intersect with yours with the intent to understand them, yourself, or the events better. When you write from a place of exploration, you don't drive the sword of blame into anyone—you open an investigation and draw the reader along for a journey of discovery.
- **PRACTICE COMPASSION.** Beyond understanding comes an even higher level of emotion. Can you find compassion for the travails of the people you are writing about, for how their suffering caused them to behave badly? Can you identify with some part of your subjects and, in the process, empathize or find some compassion for their human struggle? Even when writing about a terrible villain or a story of abuse, you still have to find a human quality within the character to make him come off as three-dimensional; every person was somebody's baby once; every villain was once a well-meaning person struggling with some burden.
- **PUT BLAME ASIDE.** When you take the stance of nonjudgment, leaving blame out of the picture, you reveal the wider circumstances. This means you'll come off less like a victim

or martyr, and the people you write about won't end up as the villains.

- **RESIST BEING THE VICTIM.** The way to elicit sympathy is not to show how bad things were but to show how you or your character negotiated, navigated, and survived difficult experiences. If you draw attention to the "woe is me" nature of terrible situations, readers won't feel pity for you. And what you want, again, is not pity, but understanding, growth, and perspective. Everyone roots for the underdog, especially when she begins to see her path as worthy of walking and presses ahead to make a better life for herself.

TABOO SUBJECTS

Beyond your personal taboos are larger taboos, cultural taboos, religious taboos. You may want to write about some dark things to shed light on them: sex trafficking, family abuse, anarchists, terrorism, incest. These aren't easy topics that everyone knows how to handle. Again, if you listen to voices that try to silence you, you are depriving the world of an opportunity to learn something new.

Here are some strategies for tackling a larger taboo.

- **KEEP IT CLOSE.** Until you know who you should ask to read your work for critique and support, don't sabotage yourself by sharing it.
- **SEEK SIMILAR WORKS.** Find other books or writers who have tackled your subject so you know you're not alone, and examine how they have handled the topic.
- **KEEP AN EYE ON THE I.** Try to draw the reader back to your own experience as much as possible, and bring empathy to bear on what you write every time so that you don't appear to be blaming or judging others.

At the end of the day, remember that your subjects, experiences, and memories belong to you.

WORK IT

Identify five to ten hot-button topics you've always thought you couldn't or wouldn't write about. Pick the scariest one, and freewrite about it for a minimum of ten minutes with the knowledge that you never have to share it with anyone. How do you feel after your freewriting is done? Excited, euphoric, scared?

Continue to move down your list of taboo topics, and complete a freewriting session for each of them. See if other topics grow organically from your original list. Eventually you may decide to share what you wrote with a trusted member of your Creative Support Team.

When you begin to freewrite about one, pick the least-charged or least-hot topic on the list and work your way up to the more intense ones. Start small.

MOVE IT

Taboos keep you small and confined. For your movement break, do one of the following big movements.

- jumping jacks
- warrior yoga pose
- windmill arm circles

PERSISTENCE IS PERSONAL
Healing Comes When We Don't Hold Back
by Rachel Thompson, best-selling author of *Broken Pieces*
and *Huffington Post* blogger

Do you have confidence in yourself, not only as a person but as a writer? I had to reach a point of confidence in myself in order to write my third nonfiction book, *Broken Pieces*. The book contains poems and essays about the sexual abuse I suffered as a child and its effects on my adult relationships, and I'm still dealing with it as I write the next book in the Broken series, *Broken Places*. I also touch on date rape, the loss of an ex to suicide, and love and loss. I didn't have a long-term plan to write about these topics, but after writing two humor books, I found myself drawn to the idea of sharing these more serious experiences. In the past, the stories had been there for so very long, patiently waiting to come out. Suddenly they weren't so patient. They were ready, pushing me, wanting to be heard.

I felt afraid—well, not so much afraid as tentative. Would anyone really be interested? Would they think that when I shared such personal stories I was being exploitative or perhaps even vain? At some point, I let all of that go and just wrote, silencing those "What if?" voices and mining deeply to find the core of each story. I felt lighter and less scared after I wrote *Broken Pieces*.

Sharing my story has connected me to an amazing survivor community that, frankly, I had no idea existed. People (mostly women, but many men as well) e-mailed or contacted me on social media with their own heartbreaking stories of childhood sexual abuse, which led me to connect with survivor, therapist, and author Bobbi Parish to start #SexAbuseChat weekly on Twitter (Tuesdays at 6 P.M. PST).

As I finish up writing *Broken Places*, I'm grateful to have such wonderful support not only from the survivor community (one in three women have experienced abuse before the age of eighteen, and one in six men) but also a large community of readers and fans who support my work.

VALIDATION

Writers, especially young writers, commonly look to others for validation: teachers, classmates, friends, or family. I was no different.

I started writing seriously in 2008, and I released my first book in 2011. In our new online society, we receive validation in the form of blog comments, retweets, Facebook or Google+ shares, and book reviews once books are published. Sometimes the comments are positive, sometimes negative.

The issue with looking to others for validation and support is that we're afraid to go too deep. We fear that people won't like what they see. In essence, we're still acting like children searching for external approval.

PERMISSION

Before we can get to the point of writing and sharing our stories, we have to first do a little work. Ask yourself what's holding you back. Typically it's one of the following reasons.

- What will my family think?
- What will my friends and co-workers think?
- What if people hate my work?
- What if I'm no good at writing?

Every writer asks herself these questions. The trick is not to let these fears prevent you from writing.

Humor is my defense. In fact, it's a form of dissociation. I wrote two nonfiction humor books that have done quite well. But it wasn't a perfect fit. Even I could tell that I wasn't going deep enough—I wasn't digging into the truth.

And then I came upon this quote by author and professor Lorrie Moore in *Elle* magazine: "The only really good piece of advice I have for my students is, 'Write something you'd never show your mother or father.'" That sentence alone, just that, was very freeing to me. Turns out I didn't need anyone's permission but my own.

If you are a writer—and you need to own that title if you are—you don't owe anyone an explanation about what you write. You are an adult. Write like one.

A FINAL WORD

Not writing your story the way you really want to is an excuse; you're feeding your insecurities. Acknowledge them. We all have them. Tie them up with a string, put them in your desk drawer, and sit down to write.

They'll still be there when you're done.

chapter 22

NOURISH YOURSELF TO AVOID BURNOUT

"If you feel burnout setting in, if you feel demoralized and exhausted, it is best, for the sake of everyone, to withdraw and restore yourself. The point is to have long-term perspective."
—DALAI LAMA

The problem with being a writer, especially if you love what you do, is that the line between work and the rest of your life is often so slender it hardly exists. Writers are often self-motivated to a fault, notoriously bad at stopping, especially if, like me, you work from home and your "office" is your portable laptop. Add in the fact that the amount of inspiration and ideas you have don't necessarily match the actual amount of time you have to work on anything, and you may find yourself always squeezing work in and around the crevices of your life.

Sometimes you'll find yourself plugging along through the work as though an invisible overlord is holding a firebrand just over your head, threatening to stamp the word *lazy* on your temple if you don't keep at it.

There is no overlord but you. If you're self-employed in any fashion, you know how easy it is to become overwhelmed by your projects, even when the pressure is self-created. Oh sure, you have deadlines and clients and book contracts, but none of those are imminent today, certainly not right this minute if your health or well-being are suffering, and even those that are most pressing could probably be granted some wiggle room if it allows you a chance to refresh and nourish.

When you reach overload, your subconscious mind probably tells you so before your conscious mind knows it. Suddenly information can no longer get in; you've reached complete saturation. The symptoms of this saturation are manifold: People who are talking to you have to repeat themselves after they catch you staring off into space. You lose your train of thought midsentence. And, if you're like me, you engage in joke-telling and other goofy steam-releasing silliness.

You might also discover the hard way that you're burned out: You get sick, fall into a cranky state that makes socializing a chore, drop the ball on your projects, and snap at people. A burned-out brain feels the way muscles do if you've worked out too hard—sore and fatigued, every push an effort.

Many writers don't schedule breaks because writing time can be hard to come by. But breaks are necessary. Crucial even. Everyone needs a break, even if only for a few minutes.

You need to stay vigilant when it comes to burnout. Yes, you can burn out even on something you love to do. A friend of mine posted recently on Facebook about the way her art can preoccupy her to the point of disregarding her physical needs, like food and rest, and make her feel depressed or anxious. You have to impose limits on yourself.

This chapter is all about ways to nourish yourself so that you can continue to be strong, present, and alive for your writing practice and your life. Fatigue, burnout, discouragement, and even just the good hard work of revision are all taxing to the creative mind and heart. You must replenish in order to fulfill your responsibilities and be available for your creative projects. Yes, the ideas may be coming so fast and furious that you may be afraid they will cease if you stop. But if you wear down the machine, it won't matter what the words are doing; you won't be able to write them.

Nonwriters don't always know or appreciate how much work writing can be. Reaching the end of a writing session can feel as if you've run a marathon or been through an intensive therapy session. It's quiet work on the outside, and thus you can't expect others to understand or provide the care you need to fill the empty well. You can't look to others to make you take care of yourself—it's up to you. What's more, when you put nourishing habits into place, you are more likely to keep up with your practice rather than simply burning down to your last bit of fuel and then having to take massive time off for recovery.

Nourishing your writer self isn't just about filling up creatively and emotionally after you've emptied out either; it's about learning how to stay ahead of that depletion so that you aren't always playing catch-up later.

KEEP QUIET

Writers thrive on quiet. Sometimes, even when my family is being absolutely still, engaged in their own projects, I swear I can feel them psychically, and that can be enough to limit my muse. I know some writers who can write to music but just as many who can't (I fall into the "can't" camp). Many writers can tune out the white noise of an anonymously public place but not the intimate or personal noise of their family. You may tell yourself you can write anywhere, and I do wish that for you, but most writers I know need a certain amount of true silence in order to get writing done. If you're a writer who works best in peace, then you must find ways to schedule it and give it to yourself. Don't set yourself up for failure by assuming you'll have a quiet spot somewhere, only to arrive and find that's not the case. Know your destinations, keep them in your pocket, and go to them time and time again. Or you may have to cut a deal with a spouse to take children out of the house, ask a roommate to alternate "work" times in your home, or reserve a room at your local library.

If you absolutely have to work around others, use a white noise app or put on your earphones and listen to a continuous kind of music that has no lyrics and moves at a slow cadence—for instance, the music massage therapists and psychologists use with their clients.

SET BREAKS

Your body is the canary in the burnout coal mine. When burnout strikes, an ailment that doesn't usually hurt will often light up, electric with pain that isn't easily quelled, or chronic pains will throb more painfully than usual. As my husband loves to quote, from Cardinal Lamberto in *Godfather III*, "The mind suffers, and the body cries out." When this happens it's time to consider whether you've been spending too many hours at the computer—and time to change your habits.

If you're not great at keeping track of time, set a timer: on your phone, on the kitchen stove, via a friend who texts you, "Stretch break!" It doesn't matter how, but your body and mind both need breaks from work, even if the work is pleasurable. Breaks are also good for stimulating fresh clarity or helping you if you're wrestling with a tough writing dilemma. Many times walking away from the writing is the best way to get the ideas flowing again.

GET MORE SLEEP

I have written into the wee hours of the night and risen as early as 5 A.M. to begin writing. I know writers who write best between 11 P.M. and 3 A.M., and others who simply stay up all night until the work is done. In order to squeeze out the time to write, some writers feel they have to carve into the time normally reserved for sleep. But let me assure you that after too long, depriving yourself of sleep will cut into your mental capacities. Studies have shown that lack of sleep has some pretty nasty cumulative effects on cognition and function. It lowers your stress threshold, impairs your mood, reduces general alertness, and dulls your creativity. Just ask new parents, who stumble and slur through the days of a newborn's introduction to the family. If you don't have enough time to both sleep and write, you're faced with an imbalance in your life somewhere, and you will have to decide the value of your writing in order to shift that balance. Your writing is dependent upon your well-being and health. Don't skimp on sleep more than once a week—find an alternative time to write instead.

GET MOVING

I'm no Jillian Michaels; I won't yell at you to get off the couch or "get after it." I don't want you to feel bad or pressured about an exercise regime. I hope that by now, after reading this far into the book, however, you know that just a little bit of exercise can make a vast difference in your brain power, your memory, your ability to learn new things, and your energy and clarity for writing. Exercise is a key component of a writing practice, whether it's practicing chair yoga at your desk or going for a good six-mile run before work. Perhaps a better way to think of it is as "movement" rather than exercise. After prolonged periods of time spent sitting, the body needs to move. After too long focused on a screen, your eyes and mind need a break, too.

Did you know that, unlike your blood, which has your heart to pump it, your lymphatic system—a key component to your immunity—has no such automatic pump to keep you healthy? It relies upon your activity to move that lymphatic fluid around and eventually out through the lymph nodes. So when you get up and walk around, dance, swing your arms, skip, or otherwise move, you're increasing mental clarity, immunity, mood, and creativity. Not bad for a few laps around the block or a dance session to your favorite song.

GO ON RETREAT

Even if you are fitting in all the writing you need to do, there's something about getting away from your everyday responsibilities and routines—particularly to a place that facilitates deep quiet—that is especially nourishing to writers. It's why places like Hedgebrook, Yaddo, Writer Path, and the like exist: because writers need immense focus and solitude. But in lieu of those big retreats, you can take yourself on small local retreats and even practice mental retreats in the following ways.

- **EYES WIDE SHUT:** Take a little time during your workday to sit with your eyes closed. I'm not even saying to meditate—simply limit the sensory input you likely receive from all those "screens" that have become a part of daily life. Tune in to your ears instead. Rub your fingers across a surface, and focus on the tactile sensation. Sip or eat something, and relish the taste. And it's not a bad idea to take some deep breaths while you're at it, focusing on the path of the breath as it slides in and out of your lungs.
- **NEGATE NOVELTY:** You've finished a project, an item on the to-do list, another page or chapter or novel. Don't rush on to the next one. Take a palate-cleansing pause to do *nothing* (with your mind, at least). Rather than jumping right in to the next item on the list, take a little stroll around the block or the office complex, or just step outside if the weather permits.
- **SMARTPHONES DUMB US DOWN:** I have a love-hate relationship with my iPhone. It keeps me connected via text and e-mail in ways I so appreciate, but ever since its introduction into my life I am aware at all times of its presence or lack thereof. I feel the need to check its face constantly, and I feel bereft if I should accidentally misplace it or leave it behind. With its ever-present source of information, it's possible that

I could never be bored again—which is wonderful for waiting at the DMV but not so great for creativity. Creativity thrives on downtime. New ideas arise from the "nothing" that comes with a lack of mental activity. So take a smartphone break. Set a time limit—and work on increasing it every week. In the first week, take a ten-minute daily break in which you don't look at your phone at all, not to e-mail or play games or take calls. Then add ten minutes each subsequent week, working up to an hour or several hours away from your phone at a time … whatever is feasible for you.

- **NATURE'S WAY:** My favorite form of retreat involves nature and getting outdoors. Now, I don't mean you have to venture far into the wild woods or up a mountain—if there are trees in your yard or neighborhood, they will do. Gardening is one of my favorite ways to rest my mind. I have spent as much as an hour watching fat carpenter bees pollinate my flowers while I soak up some early-morning sun. My birdfeeder offers another distraction as the local finches vie for a tasty morsel. If you can get to a natural spot that's also away from the sounds and scents of civilization, even better. Wind through trees, birdsong, and the gentle *whap* of wave on wave are some of the most cleansing and restorative sounds.
- **LOCAL RETREAT CENTERS:** If you want to really make a go of a true retreat, investigate retreat centers that are local to you and find out what it costs to plan your own day or weekend retreat. Often many of these places are geared to be low-cost and flexible.
- **MAKE YOUR OWN NATURE RETREAT:** If you can walk, hike, or drive quickly to a local park or open-space area, all you need is a notebook, a bag lunch, and appropriate gear for the weather, and you can make your own retreat.

- **RETREAT WITH FRIENDS:** Grab a member (or several) of your Creative Support Team, and consider renting a little house or putting up tents in a pastoral local setting. As long as you commit to truly giving yourselves downtime or time to write, the added support of a writing buddy can make an event like this more likely and more fun.

INTERCHANGE IMPRESSIONS

The work you do brings with it a series of mental "impressions"—you are, after all, creating people, their worlds, and their conflicts and holding them in your head. These impressions or images carry a sort of energy, and just like in the physical body, where repetitive motions can create "repetitive strain" or injury, I believe the mind needs a break from the same set of images, the same path. If all you're doing every day is writing an exhaustive novel, consider taking a break to read some poetry or visit a local museum. Tune into your other senses: Put on music, or even watch a quick show so long as it doesn't interfere with writing time. If nature isn't your thing, consider a spa, sports, or a café date with a friend.

KEEP PERSPECTIVE

We have ways of convincing ourselves that if the work isn't done "now," civilization as we know it will crumble; most certainly your business or project or family will, right? Nope! This just isn't true 99.9 percent of the time, especially if you schedule breaks in advance so that you, your family, your work, and your clients know when you won't be available. And even more, consider the greater plan: At the end of your life, you want to know you did your best work but in the healthiest way possible for yourself and your loved ones.

CURATE KIND WORDS

Most writers I know aren't always very kind to themselves when it comes to their writing, their talent, and their results. Perhaps you've called yourself names, denigrated your own work, compared yourself and come up short to others you think are "better." You may have even gone so far as to physically poke, pinch, prod, or slap yourself when you feel your work isn't measuring up. Every time you abuse yourself, you reinforce those negative thoughts. You are a writer, after all; words matter. They get in and can do real harm. Call yourself stupid enough times and see what happens.

It doesn't matter how you go about it, but try to surround your writing space and the front pages of notebooks with words that speak kind, empowering things to and about you. A friend of mine has taken to posting a note on her computer that says, "Be Awesome!" Another friend, Nanea Hoffman, founder of the website Sweatpants & Coffee, posted an image recently that read, "Kindness is just love with its work boots on."

Whatever words work for you and make you feel better, more inspired, and happier, put them in front of you: on the dashboard of your car, on your refrigerator, or on your coffeepot. Write them in fancy calligraphy, or type them on an old-fashioned typewriter. Post the quotes of other people who have said kind things to you. Make graphics using Photoshop or apps like Picmonkey, in which you can digitally manipulate images and photos, to post on your Facebook page or Tumblr account.

As early as 400–600 A.D. and well into the 1400s, in Italy and the Roman Empire, important books, often scriptural, were "illuminated" by monks and clergy—painted and embellished with beautiful paints, often gold and silver, and made into mini works of art. I want you to create your own illuminated words, particularly those that have an impact on you. For instance, you might really need to hear that you are

Capable or Lyrical or Accomplished. Or you may need to know that your writing is Moving, Powerful, and Evocative. Only you know what words set off that particular fizz of feeling in you.

Words are powerful because they set the foundation for your thoughts and beliefs. For more proof of the power words wield over your beliefs and sense of self, look no further than the placebo effect. Time and time again it's been shown that merely being told they are ingesting a particular medicine or "cure" can cause people to experience symptom relief even though the "medicine" is in fact a placebo—usually a benign sugar pill.

Think of these kind words as placebos that will make both you and your writing better. We are amazingly susceptible individuals—advertising has been playing on our subconscious desires and fears for decades. Consider "Just Do It," "Think Different," and "Finger Lickin' Good." So curate your own kind words. Describe to yourself the qualities you'd like to have or embody. Even better, pretend you already are those wonderful things. Start walking the walk before you arrive at your destination.

WORK IT

1. Pick a form of nourishment you're lacking, and give it to yourself when you feel signs of burnout. Arrange to go on some form of "retreat" once a month. Get an extra hour of sleep, or take a walk.

2. Create a list of words that get your blood thumping with inspiration and energy. Take some time with actual pens, crayons, glitter glue, or even just Photoshop to "illuminate" them and put them up where you can see them every time you write.

MOVE IT

What makes your body feel rejuvenated, rested, replenished? The answer is different for everyone. For a lot of people, yoga has this power. Or a warm bath. For some, an endorphin-producing activity does the trick. For others, a few minutes lying down with the sounds of the ocean playing in your earbuds can do it. If you're not sure, pick something that appeals to you, that you sense will bring you to a state of calm and peace, rest and nourishment, and include it in your weekly, if not daily, routine. Try it now.

chapter 23

GO IT ALONE:
WHEN TO SELF-PUBLISH AND PURSUE YOUR UNIQUE VISION

"Be yourself—not your idea of what you think some-body else's idea of yourself should be."
—HENRY DAVID THOREAU

Before I talk about when it's a good time to self-publish, I first want to explore what it means to be a writer with a unique vision. If you are such a writer, you might at times feel that you are a square peg in a round hole or all alone adrift at sea. At this point we've discussed developing a distinct voice and daring to be bold, claiming your skills and doing the good hard work of your chosen craft. Now we're going to talk about whether it's time to direct your skills toward self-publishing or to taking a traditional approach.

As a writer (artist!), you have a vision or you are in the process of shaping that vision, but either way you are drawn to write because of some individualized spark inside you. And just because there are many niches and slots into which most writing fits (i.e., sells), that reality does not guarantee that your writing will fit perfectly into one of them. There are always outliers and visionaries who just don't fit the mold or the times, the culture or the trends. If you are one of these writers, this doesn't make your writing bad—it makes it singular. It may mean that in order to communicate what you have to say, you can't rely on the existing infrastructure or the people you have so far relied on for your creative visions.

Let me be clear: I'm not talking about ignoring feedback that helps you improve. Ignoring feedback because the work is scary, hard, or overwhelming and then moaning that no one "gets" you is not being a visionary or an outlier; that's being timid or entitled. You may be an outlier if you hear over and over again, "Wow, this is really different," or "I've never read anything like this before," or, my personal favorite, "We just don't know how to market you." You may be a writer with a style or vision that is, as they say, ahead of the curve or before its time.

In that case, self-publishing may be a good option for you, because while the gatekeepers in publishing may not know what to do with your work, often readers are not schooled in the same genre niches or trends, and they aren't worried about any bottom line or profit making. They just want to be entertained and educated. One of the most exciting aspects of self-publishing, which many authors have discovered, is that readers are a lot more forgiving than agents and publishers. Now, that is no reason to put out halfhearted work; readers may be forgiving, but they aren't stupid. They know when a work isn't finished or the author didn't sew up all the threads. They'll notice if you've left in errors or taken shortcuts. But a publisher has wholly different demands to consider, not the least of which is whether or not they can justify making a financial investment in something they have no guarantee for. Big publishers are not known for that level of risk very often, and from a business model standpoint, you can't blame them. But you aren't likely writing from a business model standpoint, and if your writing truly falls outside the margins, then you may have entirely different considerations.

SMALL PRESS PUBLISHERS

If you feel that you truly are an outlier—that is to say, once again, you write something that just isn't in the current zeitgeist of popular subjects or styles—but you have, in fact, done all the work of revision and put a high polish on the manuscript to boot, then there's another avenue to try before you go the self-publishing route. Small presses, the labors of love of independent businesspeople who are not owned by a Big Publisher but who still follow all the legitimate processes of publishing (i.e., they pay to publish you rather than the other way around), are often hungry for talented, unusual books that the mainstream publishers are overlooking.

They may pay smaller advances, but they often invest an immense amount of personal attention and promotion to each of their authors, and many will take unagented submissions. I always recommend that writers consider these options before moving on to self-publishing.

Some great small presses I admire include:

- **DZANC BOOKS:** Unusual in the publishing industry, Dzanc Books is a nonprofit organization whose funds from sales of their books go to such endeavors as publishing a monthly online literary journal, *The Collagist*; providing low-cost writing instruction to beginning and emerging writers by connecting them with professional writers through Creative Writing Sessions; and offering a Writer-in-Residence program.
- **PRESS 53:** A small press based in North Carolina, Press 53 specializes in short story and poetry collections. They also hold contests annually, awarding a financial prize, plus publication, to the winners.
- **ENGINE BOOKS:** They are perhaps my favorite small publisher for their mission statement alone: "Big-house publishing is driven by profit. As great presses are bought up by international conglomerates, the profit burden for each title skyrock-

ets. Corporate publishers select and promote books based on potential revenues. The result is a body of relatively 'safe' literature by established writers. Big presses still publish many wonderful books, often by first-time writers; they also pass on dozens of books that deserve to be published. Engine Books demands very little profit from its titles. Though each book will be aggressively promoted to offer writers the widest possible exposure, work is selected by the quality of its storytelling and edited with an eye toward enhancing that storytelling."

Engine Books publishes only four titles per year, though they aim to expand. They also host an annual novel award, which comes with a cash prize and publication.

HYBRID PRESSES

Hybrid presses meet writers halfway. They may not pay an advance but will pay for either production of or distribution of your book. They may produce your print book while you control your e-book. They may do all the work up front but rely on print-on-demand services to produce your book instead of doing a big up-front print run, which means there's no chance for returns and no money taken from your royalties. So while you don't make up-front money, you may not have to fork over money to produce your book, and you'll benefit from their ability to feature your book in trade catalogs or online bookstores, distribute to brick-and-mortar bookstores in some cases, and even receive traditional reviews.

Examples of hybrid publishers are:

- **BOOKTROPE**: Booktrope is a hybrid publisher that works like a writer's collective. You can be accepted only through the referral of a Booktrope author. Booktrope is very interested in self-motivated writers with strong platforms and experience in self-publishing. Once accepted, you then enter "Teamtrope"—

a bit like Facebook for Booktrope's members, where you make a bid to pull together a team, including a book manager, cover designer, and marketing person, who will produce your book from within Booktrope's community of freelancers. All team members take a small percentage of the royalties from sales of your book, so your whole team is motivated to help you produce the best possible book. Booktrope uses print-on-demand technology, but through Lightning Source your books can be made available to brick-and-mortar bookstores and through all regular online outlets. Authors published with Booktrope have a tougher time qualifying for book reviews in trade publications, such as *Kirkus Reviews* or *Publishers Weekly*, though it has been done.

- **ENTANGLED PRESS.** Solely a romance publisher, Entangled works in a similar way to Booktrope, in that all staff involved in the production of a book have a financial stake in the project and split royalties with authors. As its website says, "We don't make money unless *you* make money." Authors receive royalties on cover sales, can qualify for reviews in major journals, and receive distribution all over the world through MacMillan, one of the largest print distributors in the world.

- **SHEBOOKS.** Shebooks is a digital-only publisher of 10,000-word e-books written by women. Some authors receive advances up front, while others simply get royalties, depending on negotiations. Shebooks's team edits, designs your cover, and produces each digital book. They also make the book available through online retailers and their own unique Shebooks app, which, for a monthly fee, allows subscribers unlimited access to all their books.

SELF-PUBLISHING

What's motivating you to self-publish? It's important that you identify the difference between self-publishing because what you write doesn't have an easy or comfortable niche and you want to control the rights to your work, and self-publishing because you're impatient or in a hurry or you think it requires less work. (Hint: Self-publishing requires about twenty-five times *more* work than the traditional route for the writer-publisher.)

As markets narrow and publishers take fewer risks on debut authors, and as technology improves and more people have access to better digital publishing tools, there has never been a better or easier time to self-publish. And by "easier" I mean that all the tools are at your disposal and are more sophisticated and user-friendly than ever before. It is still an enormous time commitment and financial investment to self-publish, regardless of how you do it.

To determine whether you are ready to self-publish successfully, consider the following checklist. You are ready to self-publish only when you've taken the following steps.

- You've had your book developmentally edited.
- You've had your book copy edited.
- You've decided on your top seven search-engine optimized keywords.
- You have worked those keywords into your concise, sexy "jacket copy." (This is a paragraph that will both go on your book jacket and also be used to promote it.)
- You've decided what you want your publishing "enterprise" to be called. (Self-publishing services will want to know.)
- You've obtained a Library of Congress Number. (To get one, go to authoru.org/authors-how-to-get-your-lccn-library-of-congress-number.html.)

- You've decided on a publishing service to use (e.g., CreateSpace, Lulu, BookBaby, Lightning Source).
- You've either bought a separate package of ISBN numbers from Bowker or used the free one provided by Amazon or Smashwords. (Each version of your book, e-pub and print, has its *own* number.)
- You have created a title page that includes publisher info and possibly a "the people and places in this book are fictional" disclaimer. (Feel free to borrow from what you see in other books. Also put your ISBN and Library of Congress numbers here.)
- You have hired a cover designer. (You need not just a front cover but a "full wrap." That is, this design must include the spine, back cover, and front cover. The back cover should have room for a bar code and ISBN number as well as your jacket copy.)
- You have determined the template size of your book based on whichever service you use. (Decide on a "trim" and book size. You will need to give that info to your formatter.)
- You have selected a book formatter for print and electronic files. (You will receive several files: MOBI for Kindle, ePub for Kobo and iBooks, a Word document for Smashwords, and a PDF for print files.)
- You have created a website, either by hiring someone or using a simple, free Wordpress template.
- You have activated a Twitter account (and then engaged, organically, with your followers).
- You have made a Facebook author page (and fostered, grown, and maintained it).
- You have created accounts and uploaded files to all sites you wish to sell on.

Are you tired yet? That's just the nuts and bolts. After your book is ready for publication, you must think about marketing, a subject on which there are numerous books and resources available at the click of your mouse. Marketing is a far more creative, tricky, and imperfect animal than all that comes before. There are inexpensive advertising sites, programs like Goodreads giveaways, blog tours, and publicists for hire. As much as I'd like to walk you through the steps here, marketing is so specific to your genre that no one-size-fits-all plan exists. I do, however, recommend Joel Friedlander's website, TheBookDesigner .com, for a host of resources.

Self-publishing is not for the faint of heart. That said, there are still a ton of good reasons to do it, and here are a few.

- You keep creative control and reap all the "profits" (assuming there are any).
- You can upload revisions and change covers, titles, or anything else about your book at anytime and won't have to argue with a publisher to do so.
- You can track your own sales, which helps with marketing.
- You can use social media to help you sell.
- Selling online means you don't have to sell in brick-and-mortar bookstores, which are decreasing in number now that more people purchase their books online than ever before, and which are notoriously difficult to place self-published books in anyway.
- You can control the publication date and timing of your book.

But I would be remiss if I didn't point out the other end of the equation.

- You must do all the work or have the financial resources to hire the right people to do the work for you.
- You don't get any money up front for your finished work. No one will pay you an advance (unless you get your money from crowdfunding).
- There's no guarantee that anyone will find or buy your book.
- No one will pay you back for any losses.
- It's difficult to get inexpensive distribution, and depending on your production company, some physical and online bookstores won't carry you.

- It's difficult to get your book reviewed by traditional review sources such as *Kirkus* or *Publishers Weekly* without paying for it. (And if you do pay for it, there's no guarantee of a positive review.)

At the end of the day, however, you might say the risks for traditional publishing and self-publishing aren't so different. Traditional publishing tends to have vastly better distribution, reputation, and marketing power, but that doesn't guarantee a book's success. I can tell you many sob stories of traditionally published authors whose books did not earn out their advances, whose publishers invested very little marketing funds, and whose books thus flopped.

Self-publishing has to be worth it to you, just as your writing practice has to be worth it to you, for the love of the art, for the desire to put your words into people's hands. Just like any other part of the process, if you don't take pleasure in this part of the journey, self-publishing will be a long grind and a disappointment. You love your writing practice, remember? You have committed to yourself. Don't put yourself in a situation that will cause you to fall out of love with it. If self-publishing seems like too much right now, give it time. Go slowly, and keep trying the mainstream channels.

WORK IT

Now that you have an honest view of what it takes to self-publish, make yourself a pros-and-cons sheet. If you think you're up to the task, create a time line for yourself with the awareness that many of the tasks, from copy editing to formatting, require weeks if not months. You are most likely to have success at self-publishing if you create a business plan and a six- to twelve-month time line for your first book. (The time line can get shorter with subsequent books, but you need to be realistic your first time through.) Start investigating marketing plans now. Get your team in place.

PERSISTENCE IS PERSONAL
Going It Alone
Hugh Howey, best-selling author of *Wool* and many others

You've written your masterpiece. You've workshopped it with a writing group. Friends and family and even a few strangers have told you that this is a great work and worthy of publication. And then a pile of rejection letters from literary agents tell you that it's not right for them.

But maybe it's right for readers.

The decision to self-publish isn't easy. In fact, it can be agonizing. The first novel I ever wrote was published with a small paying press. When I got my contract for book two, I faced a painful decision. Should I stick with someone who would pay me a little but then own my work and have complete control of it? Or did I want to see how far I could take it on my own?

After much internal debate and many conversations with loved ones, I decided to maintain ownership of my hard work and go it alone. The tools and platforms that allowed me to control my own destiny had finally matured and opened up. Self-publishing today is an extremely valid path for launching a writing career. That doesn't mean there are any guarantees or that luck won't play a huge role; it just means you don't have to get stuck with zero chance. You can improve your odds.

Not publishing your book will have predictable results. So will publishing your work poorly. But here's something else to consider: Submitting your work to an agent in rough-draft form will lead to rejection as well. These days, many aspiring writers are paying to have their work professionally edited before they query agents. The same seriousness should apply however you decide to publish.

Think of self-publishing like starting up a band. You've got the skills to play an instrument, and now you're going to try to turn this into a paying career. You start on street corners with an open guitar case. You move up to small gigs in bars. You play on your first stage. You hope to build a following and maybe attract attention from a recording studio.

Writing now provides the same path to success. It means long hours and complete dedication. Most writers will give up before they master their craft, just as most musicians will never play through bleeding fingers and develop the callouses they need. But if you are part of the fraction of a single percent who will persist, who will write ten novels before they care how their sales are doing, you have a chance. Most won't do this.

Before you publish, consider the investment in time you made in writing your work. Now consider investing some money. Not in a company that will scam you, but in creating a beautiful work you will own for the rest of your life. It can be difficult to hear that you should spend $1,000 editing your work and buying stellar cover art, but there are two ways to think about this that might help.

The first is that this isn't an expensive hobby. People spend far more on whatever they fancy doing in their spare time. The difference with your book is that it can earn some of that money back. Maybe all of it. Maybe even more.

The second way to look at this is as though you're starting a small business. This book will be for sale for the rest of your life. For the e-book version, you won't have to spend a penny to create more copies of this work. It could be ten years from now that it begins to pay off. What other small business can you start for such a low investment and with such long-term benefits? I can't think of a single one.

Whether you view your writing as a hobby or as a potential career, the initial investment is crucial. Put a jar on your desk, and add a dollar for every hundred words you write. That might be five dollars a day, which means giving up a coffee or even your cable television. Watch the words and that fund build together. Let it motivate you to get through to the end. And when you decide that self-publishing is right for you, invest in your work in order to invest in yourself.

Then do it all over again.

chapter 24

WRITE OUTSIDE THE BOX

"Writing practice brings us back to the uniqueness of our own minds and an acceptance of it. We all have wild dreams, fantasies, and ordinary thoughts. Let us feel the texture of them and not be afraid of them. Writing is still the wildest thing I know."

—NATALIE GOLDBERG, FROM *WILD MIND: LIVING THE WRITER'S LIFE*

For those who have trepidation about the craft of writing, there are many answers, formulas, courses, books, and paths already laid down for you. But the known path is not the one artists tread. The work you do that ventures somewhere new, crosses new divides, and bears your singular mark may not be anywhere near those tried-and-true variables already in place.

Real art pushes outside of comfortable zones and introduces new vision. It falls "outside the box."

"The Box," of course, changes all the time. Every few years, new trends, new methods, and new approaches crop up and start running the show, and since the onset of digital publishing, I'd say these trends and methods are changing faster than ever. Sometimes writing that no one would publish a decade ago is now the hot new ticket. But the fact is, if you try to write to trends or popularity, you run the risk of driving yourself crazy.

And yet, you have inspired stories to tell. You have a distinctive viewpoint. You come with experiences remarkable to you. Those things don't always fit the mold. It's easy to feel as though there's only one way and that veering off the beaten path will lead to failure. *False!* By now I hope I've driven home that there is no such thing as failure in a writing practice. There is quitting; there are experiments that yield new fruit; there are experiments that prove to be dead-ends. But you don't fail by trying new things. You don't fail by looking outside the box. In fact, outside the box is the realm of wild and innovative success. Just at the edges of what's accepted lies new information, new ways of seeing.

"The Box" may not be what's popular but a space you've drawn to limit yourself. It's a box that says, "I can't write *that*," or "I'm a novelist; I can't write memoir." Keeping yourself within a box may be your way of unwittingly holding back from something you really want to write, that could stretch you or even be your perfect medium. I recall hearing Neil Gaiman speak at San Jose State University several years ago. He was about to read from his wildly anticipated novel *The Graveyard Book.* He said that he kept waiting to be a talented-enough writer to write the story. Every few years he would try to write it and say, "No, I'm not there yet." And then, one day, he realized he would never be as talented as he wanted to be to write it, and he just had to write it anyway.

Take Gaiman's advice: Write it anyway.

ADMIT THE OBSTACLE

So what to do about these boxes and their notoriously prohibitive qualities? First, of course, you have to admit that the box is an obstacle. Doing so helps you identify it. For example, say you are a literary writer in terms of style, and you love to write plot. Maybe you'd like to delve into writing plot-driven fiction, but you fear that you won't be any good at it or that literary writers "just don't write those kinds of novels."

In fact, for years, plot-driven novels that were also considered literary works weren't a "thing" in the realm of fiction. You either wrote literature or you wrote genre work. And then, somewhere along the way, literary writers like Justin Cronin and Benjamin Percy started turning their keen sensibilities toward the telling of ripping good yarns. Now the literary thriller, the literary vampire novel, and a whole other host of literary crossover writing is not only accepted but sells quite well.

If you find yourself doubting that you can write cross-genre work, take some time to investigate what's already out there and see if you can't find a writer to emulate in terms of the risks or crossover they've made. Or maybe in reading this chapter you've had an *aha* moment and realized that you don't write straight out of an existing mold. If that's the case, embrace that epiphany and break new ground.

IDENTIFY YOUR DESIRE

In addition to recognizing and admitting that the box is an obstacle to your forward success, you must also ask yourself what you're yearning to write but don't feel permission to write. Are you boxing yourself in because of one of the fears we discussed in an earlier chapter? Are you holding yourself back because of internal taboos? Go back and reread those chapters to work through your fears and hang-ups. Often you've kept yourself inside the box simply because it's accepted as the common denominator, the preference of the masses. It's all that you know.

But what else would you like to write? How else would you like to go about it? What would you write if there were no restrictions—internal or external? One of the most transformative writers I read in graduate school was Italo Calvino, an Italian surrealist whose writing is a hybrid of short story and prose poetry. His words paint visuals that linger in the mind. Are there plots and character arcs? Not that I can find. These stories don't lend themselves to literal interpretation, but much like dreams, they provide an impressionistic, even hallucinatory, series of images you can add up any way your mind perceives. My favorite of Calvino's books is *Invisible Cities*, the story of the historical figure Marco Polo on his journeys, in conversation with the Emperor Kublai Khan. His journeys take him through magic "cities," each different and fantastical, and a metaphor for some aspect of Polo's journey.

> You walk for days among trees and among stones. Rarely does the eye light on a thing, and then only when it has recognized that thing as the sign of another thing: a print in the sand indicates the tiger's passage; a marsh announces a vein of water; the hibiscus flower, the end of winter. All the rest is silent and interchangeable; trees and stones are only what they are. Finally the journey leads to the city of Tamara. You penetrate it along streets thick with signboards jutting from the walls. The eye does not see things but images of things that mean other things: pincers point out the tooth-drawer's house; a tankard, the tavern; halberds, the barracks; scales, the grocer's. Statues and shields depict lions, dolphins, towers, stars: a sign that something—who knows what—has as its sign a lion or a dolphin or a tower or a star.

I have no doubt that if Calvino had tried to write inside only one box, he'd have been a bored, repressed writer.

Be honest with yourself, especially if you're feeling confined, bored, or constricted by existing "trends" and "niches." You don't have to share any of your experiments outside the box, but there's creative value in allowing yourself to venture into these places.

VENTURE BEYOND THE MARKET

Here is the conundrum of great writing: If you write *only* with the market or audience in mind, you run the risk of producing formulaic, derivative work. If you never think about your market or audience, then you may have a steeper uphill climb when it comes time to publish. But I like to think there is an in-between space called WriterLand, an alchemist's workshop where ideas hatch and mingle and form chimeras of form and genre. It's the place of creation where you don't need to worry about any boxes, because they don't exist. The writing process at its wildest is one of unlimited potential. You begin to limit your visions the moment you start writing them down, but you limit them the most when you start worrying about who's watching, listening, and so on.

So eventually, yes, you can worry about the markets, but while you're in your mad-scientist lab, let loose—leap past boundaries and constrictions and write from a wild place. You may not know what these wild excursions will produce that can be applied to later work, too. Just as repetitive motions can cause injury in the body, I believe that too much repetition of material or form can cause a writer's muse to stagnate.

FIND YOUR NICHE

As your voice forms cohesion and you settle into a clear idea of what you love to write and how this best suits your needs as a writer, you may at first think that a niche doesn't exist for your work. The mainstream bookshelves are getting ever narrower. For instance, I know plenty of female writers who write about women, family, domestic life, and sex but feel no communion with women's fiction, chick-lit, or erotica in any of its forms. You have to look beyond the top layer. The biggest publishers will go with the most reliable forms, those that take the fewest risks and hew the closest to formulas. But there is an entire counterculture of literature produced by small presses, hybrid presses, literary councils, university presses, author's collectives, and so on. And for every area of human interest, there are people who want to read about it. You can't rely upon existing forms to provide you with the path to these places. You have to discover it. You need to do some research, and along the way you may find an entire world of people and subjects opens up to you.

From fan fiction to Bigfoot erotica (not making that one up!) to LGBT literature and literature of social change, "There are more things in heaven and earth … than are dreamt of in your philosophy," as Shakespeare wrote. Sometimes going outside the box means going beyond your own understanding and learning more about options and opportunities that were previously unknown to you. And like the bewildered and sometimes terrified hero in any good story, you may experience tremors of fear, but they are worth pushing past.

WORK IT

Research something that has always interested you with the goal of bringing it into something you're working on or using it as a prompt for a new piece of writing. Watch a documentary, hole up in a library carrel with an encyclopedia or a biography, read interviews of authors you're unfamiliar with, or research photographs that fascinate you. The topics, words, and media that hold your rapt attention often make for compelling writing.

PERSISTENCE IS PERSONAL
Beyond the Box
by Heather Fowler, author of *Elegantly Naked in my Sexy Mental Illness*
and three other books

What's really strange about moving outside "the Box" is that I never even knew what the main writer's box looked like until long after I'd attained two degrees. In college, most creative writing workshops stressed the mastering of short fiction. Workshopping a novel was discouraged. Stories were revered. Naturally I thought it was okay, and, in fact, not a bad idea, to write tons and tons of short stories.

My form considerations were also influenced by a busy lifestyle. As a parent with a full-time job, shorter works were easier to undertake than novels. They fit my tiny writing windows. I wrote several hundred and published many. Nonetheless, several years later, without a published book to my name, in conversation with other writer friends, I realized that a novel would give me better traction for both money and greater field visibility. So, *Yes, yes, a novel*, I thought. *No more stories.*

I am embarrassed to admit that once I accepted this idea—a novel or bust—my writing stopped. Feeling uninspired and defeated, I couldn't seem to do it anymore.

The box and its outlines got very clear then: To get an agent and be seen, what I really needed was exactly *the* thing I could not entice myself to write. As a result, I lost faith in the endeavor of being a writer and devalued my own stories. I'd been clearly told by colleagues that only the novel mattered—because, unless I published in *The New Yorker*, honey, stories didn't count anywhere, and they "weren't what readers wanted." I was also told that stories, while great for agent-hunt bio building, were largely irrelevant for earning advances. Story collections weren't seen as viable books unless they included contest winners, and they were definitely harder to sell.

I wanted to die that year. In privacy. Preferably while cursing loudly.

Luckily, common sense soon returned. There is not just one path, I reminded myself, and I lit that novels-only box on fire, deciding that I wanted to write stories because I enjoyed writing stories, so I would first do that—and then I would put them on the market! I would send them out as collections, Novel Box be damned, because I was only languishing when I didn't work on or believe in what I wanted to write. No one profited if I stopped writing altogether, and I had to go my own way.

When I did this with my whole heart, soon enough, a story collection was accepted—this after more than a decade with no book. Within five years of actively championing my short work, I had four story collections accepted by three publishers—all this before acquiring an agent. Incidentally, once the pressure left, I wrote that novel, too. And the funny thing was, despite their supposed purpose in the agent hunt, my stories helped me secure my current agent—but this had nothing to do with "the Box" or the venue in which my stories appeared. It had everything to do with my agent taking a chance on my novel because she had faith in my short work.

That said, my message now to aspiring writers is simple: Know what the Box is supposed to be, yes, but move toward what moves you regardless. Write what's necessary to your voice as an author, and the shape of your career will feel both urgent and poignant, will emerge almost without conscious intervention. Boxless for years now, I currently find myself amazed by the directions in which the artistic impulse has taken me—and I'm grateful.

I did not anticipate these books, these stories, that arrived like pilgrims at my door. They asked only that I listen, caretake, and record.

I also had no idea, starting out as an experimental feminist literary author, that life would take my book path to magical realism first, then dystopia, then mental-illness fiction, and then ghosts, carting along poetry all the while. But my books chose me when I chose them.

I get out of their way now. I do what they say.

I no longer see a box but instead a series of doors. Whichever is most charming in any given moment is the door I crack.

chapter 25

SUBMIT STRONG

....

"This manuscript of yours that has just come back from another editor is a precious package. Don't consider it rejected. Consider that you've addressed it 'to the editor who can appreciate my work' and it has simply come back stamped 'Not at this address.' Just keep looking for the right address."

—BARBARA KINGSOLVER

....

This year, my friend and fellow author Julia Park Tracey proclaimed she no longer would use the words *submit* and *accepted* in regard to seeking publication for her work, because they spoke the language of her old self-judgments and made her feel bad. Instead she says, "I put forth my work for publication, and it is either received or not."

These subtle semantics may seem like no big deal, even silly, but think about how deeply words get lodged into your psyche, like little, dark beasts waiting to feast upon your weaknesses. Week after week you *submit* your work. What images does this word call to mind? Supplication? Falling at the feet of a superior and begging for approval? Likewise you don't need to wait for *acceptance* from others. You accept your work already; that's why you sent it out to seek publication in the first place. If it doesn't find publication, you return to my original dictate: Go deeper, or go elsewhere.

When you're ready to seek publication, play with the semantics in your own mind, because they do, in fact, make a difference.

TALK THE TALK

By the time you're submitting work, you want to present the face of a professional who has confidence in what you've written. Agents, editors of literary magazines, and publishers are looking not only for quality work but for signs that the writer moves with confidence through the world. When I edit query letters for my clients, I regularly remove phrases that say things such as: "I would be so grateful if you'd read ..." or "I hope you don't mind taking the time to read ..." or "Since I'm new at this ..."

Those lines meet my red pen quicker than you can say, "Cut," because they come across as needy, uncertain, and unconfident.

Now I'm not saying you will always feel confident, but try to drum up those kind, empowering words discussed in chapter twenty-two, "Nourish Yourself to Avoid Burnout," and talk about yourself and your work as though it holds great merit and demonstrates you know your stuff. Readers on the other end don't know how you feel inside—they know only what they read, so make your first impressions strong ones.

DO YOUR RESEARCH

Part of talking that talk means that you investigate and research every outlet you're pursuing so that you know the answers to the following questions.

- What is the tone and style of the outlet?
- Who else has been published or represented by the person, organization, or journal? (And do you feel that you fit in with that company?)

- What are the submission guidelines (including how to format your work and where to put your contact information)?
- What specific criteria is the agent, editor, or literary journal seeking? (Be sure yours meets that criteria or style.)
- How do you submit it (with or without attachment, to an e-mail address, via an online contact form, etc.)?
- What are the fees associated with your submission? If fees apply, do you want to pay for what you're submitting? (Contests and grant applications are usually the only worthy outlets to pay to be read.)

Nothing weeds out a writer's work faster than simple oversights. It's worth the extra time it takes to work through your writing and submission package with that fine-tooth comb to be sure that you've followed the specifics exactly. What writers often don't know is that while your submission is a precious singularity to you, it may be one of hundreds showing up on the other end. Therefore, tired and often overwhelmed slush-pile readers are looking for reasons to send a work packing. Don't give them that reason. Stand out, speak strong, and talk about your work in clear, firm terms.

AVOID TOO MUCH OF A GOOD THING

On the other end of the self-deprecating newbie writer is the writer who, in trying to put on a strong front, goes a little too far in her self-praise. Saying something like "I'm sending you my magnificent, heartwarming, hilarious, breathtaking novel" or "I'm a talented, innovative writer" may sound good while you're typing it, but to an agent or editor such self-praise may come across as working too hard to prove a point. If you're serious, talented, and innovative, that will probably come through in the work. And the writing must speak for itself. The trick is to believe and feel your own worth but to communicate only professionalism and to ride the current between lack of confidence and megalomania.

PICK AND CHOOSE

Say you're looking for an agent. You go to Publishers Marketplace or visit Chuck Sambuchino's *Guide to Literary Agents* blog, and you make a list that's one hundred names long. Sure, you could submit to everyone seeking "new voices"—no hard-and-fast rule says you can't. But before you do, consider a couple of things. First, recall chapter eight, "Go Where You Are Welcome." In that chapter, I suggested you pay attention to the signs that tell you an opportunity is right. In lieu of being sure of that, what you have are clear variables, usually outlined in the form of submission guidelines and "what we're looking for" links. Just because an agent is interested in "strong new voices" doesn't necessarily mean that agent is right for you. Take a look at his client list, submission criteria, and bio. Do you see a fit? If not, then consider he's probably looking for "strong new voices" of a particular kind that may not be yours and to submit your work might be a waste of time.

The goal in submitting your work is not to send it out scattershot to the wind like a handful of wildflower seeds but to pick and choose the right people with whom you resonate and feel *sympatico*, and who seem most capable of taking your work where you feel it should go.

AVOID URGENCY

I understand that at times you want to be published so intensely that the notion preoccupies you. You send your stories or novel queries out in big chunks to anyone and anywhere, reasoning that the more you throw out there the better the chances that something will stick.

But stop for a second and think about this strategy. What intention are you setting for yourself and your work? What message are you running with? That being published anywhere is better than being published in the right places? That's not true. You want to be published in the right places, by those who love and appreciate your work. You want to find your literary tribe, your compadres, your professional version of your Creative Support Team. When you find a true fit for your writing, you will never, ever want to scattershot your work again. What you want is to see your work in places you admire and to form partnerships with agents and publishers who champion and push you to be your best. Because believe me, you may hear yes from places that don't convey the vision you have for your work. I've heard the story more times than I can count (and, honestly, it's happened to me, too) of people who signed with the first agent who would "have them." They went on to regret it because it wasn't an informed and aligned choice. Just like you wouldn't want to settle for a mate, don't put yourself in the position to settle because you believe it's better than nothing. You and your work are worth more than that. Believe in yourself and your work. Go deeper, or go elsewhere.

WORK IT

Identify your dream agent, publisher, or publishing situation. List ten qualities you desire in this scenario, such as focused attention, experience with historical fiction, or comfort with frequent e-mail communication. *Then* begin your search with these specific criteria in mind. Invest in a one-month Publishers Marketplace subscription ($25), which allows you to search databases of agents and their sales via specific criteria.

MOVE IT

What exercise makes you feel the opposite of being "in submission"? For me it's when I do some low-level weight lifting. As a woman, feeling strong is important to me, so even working with some handheld weights can do the trick. What about you? Pick something that conjures a feeling of power, and do it now or whenever you're not feeling confident.

AFTERWORD

So you've come to the end of this book—now what? If you take away only one piece of advice, let it be this: The most successful writers are not preternaturally talented or perfectly poised; they are simply *persistent*. And persistence means you don't ever give up. You may take breaks or time away, but if you are persistent, your writing practice will be much deeper and wider than you first realized, and it will reanimate when you return your attention to it. It's as unique as you, and it's flexible to change, play, and redesign for the rest of your life.

There is always another avenue or side trail off the main path of your practice. I love the design of this cover, which came about after I'd already written the content. Let the image of the path that leads to that bountiful tree be a metaphor for your writing practice: As long as your roots run deep and you keep climbing, you will eventually reach fruition. It may not look as you hoped or planned, but it may be better, wilder, and grander if you just stick with it.

Most of all, remember that if you are having a bad writing day, it's only one day; focus on your body instead—move it, shake it loose, learn something new, distract yourself—and then come back to the page and start again.

Consider no effort wasted.

Keep writing.

Most importantly: Be persistent.

ABOUT THE AUTHOR

Jordan E. Rosenfeld is the author of the novels *Forged in Grace* and *Night Oracle*, as well as the writing guides *Make a Scene* and *Write Free: Attracting the Creative Life*, with Rebecca Lawton. In fall 2015 Writer's Digest Books will publish *Writing Deep Scenes*, co-authored with Martha Alderson.

Jordan is the managing editor of the popular online magazine *Sweatpants & Coffee* and a contributing editor to the nonprofit website Role/Reboot. Her articles, essays, and stories have been published in or are forthcoming at *Alternet*; *Brain, Child*; *Full Grown People*; *Literary Mama*; *HuffPost Parents*; *The Manifest-Station*; *Medium*; *Mommyish*; *The Nervous Breakdown*; *Night Train*; *The New York Times*; Ozy.com; *The Rumpus*; *San Francisco Chronicle*; *The St. Petersburg Times*; *The Washington Post*, *Writer's Digest*; and *The Writer*.

Visit her blog at www.JordanRosenfeld.net.

Check out her writing retreats with Martha Alderson at www.WriterPath.com.

INDEX